DIABLO®

THE OFFICIAL COOKBOOK

DIABLO®

THE OFFICIAL COOKBOOK

RECIPES AND TALES FROM THE INNS OF SANCTUARY

ANDY LUNIQUE | RICK BARBA

INSIGHT
EDITIONS

SAN RAFAEL · LOS ANGELES · LONDON

CONTENTS

FOREWORD

I am one of the scribes from an incredibly talented team of writers who shaped the world, characters, and stories of Sanctuary for *Diablo IV*. When I started working on Diablo, I expected to be contributing to telling a tale of loss, and of those broken by hardship and the monsters eager to rip them to shreds. However, I soon learned it was a story of the courage and humanity it takes to face the darkness, and the light within all of us.

The bonds of community can be found in the wet, werewolf-infested plains of Scosglen, or in the beautiful oasis towns of Kehjistan. Diablo reminded me that the small moments of comfort by a crackling fire are the most important. These are the moments worth fighting for in a world filled with bloodthirsty beasts lurking in every shadow.

The inhabitants of Sanctuary find these moments of solace in inns, public houses, and taverns—places to rest after trekking muddy paths for days on end and to savor every bite of a nourishing meal after fighting demons. They raise their mugs to the family and friends lost along the way, toasting the joy of living to see another sunrise.

While bartenders and locals may boast and bicker about their hometown pub serving the best mead, a room full of laughter and chatter is all anyone needs to remember they are not alone, and to forget their troubles even if for a night. Whether it's the innkeeper of Farobru serving stiff drinks to farmers, or the denizens of Marowen enjoying a fresh, roasted fish, the many flavors of Sanctuary vary from place to place. But one thing remains the same: They are all delicious.

I hope these mouthwatering recipes collected from across the lands can bring these moments of peace and coziness into your own kitchen. So, stay awhile and listen, won't you?

See you in Sanctuary.

—ALANNA CARROLL NARRATIVE DESIGNER

INTRODUCTION

Greetings, wanderers.

My mother, Nyami, was an herb merchant and a highly regarded cook. As a lad, I watched the sorriest drunkards, cutthroats, and lost souls drag themselves through the doors of Caldeum's inns, each the portrait of lost hope. With a flash of coin, she placed before them warmed legs of turkey and mutton, jellies and custards dyed with saffron and sandalwood, fritters and stews spiced with caraway and cardamom. Even if all they could afford was a trencher of pottage and a mug of ale, my mother saw them walk away warmed and ready for whatever darkness awaited them beyond her table.

The Cathedral of Light, the Zakarum, and all the others can keep their faiths. My mother deemed the kitchen her altar, and cooking a sacred art. According to her, the way one prepares a barley stew can damn or save one's soul. She imparted her knowledge to me, and, in my own way, I suppose I have followed in her footsteps.

Innkeepers across Sanctuary know me as Tedric of the Table, for I have spent decades traversing these lands, despite the peril, sampling the foods at various tables. I believe food is, at the very least, small comfort in tumultuous times. At the most, it is an expression of our history, and it stitches together the fabric of a community. The right combination of spices can transport a weary traveler to their distant homeland, while a warm meal in the belly of a foot soldier can sway a battle right.

Thus, for many years, from Khanduras to Xiansai to the Dry Steppes, I have sampled the fare of inns, public houses, and taverns, high and low. I have had the good fortune to explore the spiceries of wealthy kings, and to dine at the tables of great scholars. If I taste something that delights, surprises, or even simply comforts me, I am relentless in prying its secrets from the one who prepared it.

This book you hold is culled from my travels across Sanctuary. In these dark times, it may not be as valuable as sword or spear, or that rare capacity of rallying the dead, but I guarantee you this—the recipes nestled within these pages will bring you untold riches of *taste*.

Along with these recipes, I have also learned two important truths:

First: Good food is quite often simple food. The cook at the Slaughtered Calf Inn in New Tristram once told me that his guiding principle was to "rely on three or four savory ingredients to do the heavy lifting. Then, get out of their way."

Second: Something about sharing a revitalizing meal opens people up to sharing their stories, leading to comity, good will, and fellowship. You can learn a lot about someone over a warm plate.

While delicious food may not defeat demons, it is an excellent place to find peace.

—TEDRIC of the TABLE

INGREDIENTS GUIDE

The goal is to ensure that these recipes are inclusive and enjoyable. I encourage you to approach these dishes openly as they are safe for substitutions and adjustments. With careful consideration around experimentation, you can fit each of these dishes to meat-free, gluten-free, dairy-free, or vegan dietary needs. Here are some examples you can consider:

DAIRY:

Almond, soy, coconut, or oat milk as non-dairy milk alternatives.

Vegan cheese or nutritional yeast as a cheese alternative.

Coconut cream or non-dairy yogurt as a substitute for sour cream.

CHICKEN:

Tofu, tempeh, or seitan as a plant-based protein alternative.

Portobello mushrooms or eggplant as a meat substitute in stir-fries, curries, and stews.

Jackfruit as a shredded meat alternative in tacos and sandwiches.

BEEF:

Mushrooms or lentils for a meaty texture in burgers, meatloaf, and chili.

Textured vegetable protein (TVP) or seitan as a ground beef alternative.

Cauliflower or butternut squash as a beef substitute in stews and casseroles.

FISH:

Hearts of palm as a substitute for crab or tuna in salads and sandwiches.

Tofu or tempeh as a substitute for fish in stir-fries and curries.

King oyster mushrooms or jackfruit as a substitute for fish in fish and chips.

SHELLFISH:

Hearts of palm as a substitute for crab or lobster in salads and sandwiches.

Oyster mushrooms or eggplant as a substitute for scallops in pasta dishes.

Tofu or tempeh as a substitute for shrimp in stir-fries and curries.

GLUTEN:

Gluten-free flour such as rice, almond, or coconut flour as a substitute for wheat flour in baked goods.

Quinoa, rice, or corn pasta as a substitute for wheat pasta.

Tamari or aminos as a substitute for soy sauce in marinades and dressings.

RECIPE SKILL LEVELS

Cooking is a skill and, for some, a vocation. All the Sanctuary recipes I've culled for you from my travels were developed by seasoned chefs across the lands. But please note that many of these dishes are quite easy to prepare, even if you're new to the kitchen. For guidance, I've given every recipe one of the following difficulty levels:

APPRENTICE

Recipes marked as Apprentice level are easy to prepare . . . and yet, trust me, they still end up as extraordinary fare. Dishes like New Tristram Braised Greens, Hoodwinked Honey Carrots, or Exiled Eggplant Dip may sound intimidating but are remarkably simple to make . . . even if you've never touched an ingredient in your life!

JOURNEYMAN

Recipes at this level feature more steps and often call for some light skills—for example, special handling of certain ingredients, or the application of specific cooking techniques. Captain's Crew Fish Stew, Reshomi's Spiced Shortbread, and Bandit's Bacon Candy are examples of dishes that call for this Journeyman level of skill.

ARTISAN

Dishes like Wessel's Venison Stew, Owl Tribe Shredded Beef, and Gray Wards Onion Pie call for a somewhat wider range of cooking skills—better proficiency with knives, for example, or comfort with juggling concurrent tasks.

MASTER

Recipes designated Master level are decidedly more difficult and time-consuming to prepare. These dishes typically include many steps, sometimes with tricky timing and less room for error, requiring careful focus and attention. It certainly helps to know your way around a kitchen when preparing, say, Highlands Rabbit Fricassee or the amazing Lauded Laminated Pancakes. But again, don't be afraid! I guarantee that every Master-level recipe is well worth the extra effort.

THE SLAUGHTERED CALF INN

NEW TRISTRAM, KHANDURAS

In a rugged land riven by conflict, the Slaughtered Calf Inn endures. Whether serving up a scrumptious beef bourguignon or a spice-rubbed leg of mutton, this New Tristram mainstay has always fulfilled the promise of its moniker. A steadfast shelter amid the darkness that has enveloped Khanduras, the inn has long offered its patrons comforting food and strong ale . . . at least, strong enough to help one forget the risen dead roaming the area.

During my time there, the face of the Slaughtered Calf was its proprietor and barkeep, Bron. From my own youth, I remember Bron as fine a conversationalist as any I have met in these dark lands . . . quickly recalling his patrons' favorite dishes, even as his hands struggled to keep up with travelers who seemed younger and younger with each passing year.

When last I saw him, Bron had hired Othyrus to help him with daily upkeep of the inn, and Othyrus was every bit as good at tossing together a coq au vin as Bron was at brewing the finest ale in Khanduras. It was over several mugs of the Slaughtered Calf's best brew that Bron shared the enclosed recipes.

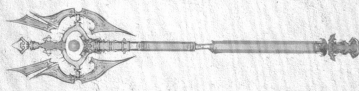

OTHYRUS'S VEGETABLE RISOTTO

I doubt there exists a soul in Sanctuary who has not suffered at the hands of a bandit or cutpurse; one of my many turns came about one morning outside New Tristram. As I plodded past a thick copse of trees, a trio of brigands ambushed me, threatening to gut me like a fish if I refused to hand over my coin. When I stumbled into a dark corner of the Slaughtered Calf Inn afterwards with my pockets empty, the barmaid, Eira, took one look at me and served a bowl of Othyrus's vegetable risotto. "Eat this," she said. "Sprigs of rosemary are good for the body." She grinned and added, "And I'll draw a stout ale to soothe your soul."

Difficulty: Artisan
Prep/Cook: 40 to 50 minutes
Yield: 4 servings

7 cups broth (chicken or vegetable)
1 bay leaf
⅛ teaspoon saffron threads
3 sprigs rosemary
8 ounces sliced button mushrooms
4 garlic cloves, minced
1 tablespoon unsalted butter, melted
8 ounces parsnips, peeled and diced
1 tablespoon extra-virgin olive oil
1 cup pearl barley
1 onion, finely chopped
½ cup dry white wine
1 cup heavy cream
6 ounces frozen peas
2 teaspoons chopped fresh thyme
1 cup shredded Parmesan cheese
Chopped fresh parsley or chives
3 tablespoons sunflower seeds

1. In a large stock pot, bring the broth to a boil. Add the bay leaf, saffron, and rosemary sprigs.

2. Clean and slice the mushrooms. Be sure they remain dry.

3. In a medium pan, sauté the mushrooms with the minced garlic until tender. Set aside.

4. Sauté the parsnips with the melted butter. Remove, and mix with the mushrooms.

5. Add the olive oil to the pan, and then add the barley.

6. Lightly toast the barley on medium heat until a light golden-brown color coats the grain, about 3 to 4 minutes.

7. Add in the onion and cook until fragrant, about 1 minute.

8. Add the wine to the pan, and quickly deglaze the barley around the pan with a wooden spoon. Stir, and continue to cook for 2 minutes or until most of the liquid is gone.

9. Using a ladle, add 8 ounces of the warm stock to the barley. Keep on stirring and simmering until all the liquid is absorbed; then add the next 8 ounces. About 2 to 3 minutes of cooking and stirring are needed per ladle of broth. (Note: This normally takes longer than cooking rice.)

10. Repeat until all the stock is used or until the barley is creamy but maintains a bit of chew, about 15 to 20 minutes total.

11. When the barley is tender, add the heavy cream and frozen peas, and stir until slightly reduced, about 2 minutes. Then pour the mixture into a large bowl, to make mixing easier.

12. In the large mixing bowl, add the cooked mushrooms, parsnips, thyme, Parmesan cheese, and parsley, and then mix well.

13. Spoon barley into bowls, and top with sunflower seeds.

OLD TRISTRAM TOASTED PILAF

As my mother used to say, flavor and scent can extricate a trove of memory. Othyrus traced the origin of this pilaf recipe back to Old Tristram, prior to King Leoric's descent into madness and the Darkening of Tristram. The old town was a lively place then, when nobody knew what festered in the catacombs beneath Leoric's chosen seat of power. I find this simple, barley-based recipe a mood-lifting preamble to any meal—one that reminds me of the promise this land once held . . . and the ghosts that dine at its table.

Difficulty: Journeyman
Prep/Cook: 30 minutes
Yield: 4 servings

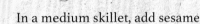

2 tablespoons sesame oil

2 shallots, thinly sliced

1 cup pearl barley

½ teaspoon white pepper

1 teaspoon ground coriander

¼ teaspoon Chinese five-spice powder

1 tablespoon table salt

2½ cups vegetable broth

1 cup ripe pear, peeled, cored, and cut into ½-inch dice

⅔ cup chopped walnuts

1 tablespoon salted butter

1. In a medium skillet, add sesame oil and cook shallots over medium heat for 5 minutes or until softened.

2. Add barley; cook and stir for 5 minutes, allowing the kernels to toast.

3. Stir in pepper, coriander, and five-spice and cook for 1 minute until fragrant.

4. Add broth and bring to a boil; reduce heat and simmer, covered, for 40 minutes or until barley is tender and chewy.

5. Stir in diced pears and allow the residual heat to soften the pears. Cover and let stand for 10 minutes.

6. Remove from heat and stir in walnuts, butter, and salt and serve.

BRON'S BEEF BOURGUIGNON

You never know who could be passing through the Slaughtered Calf Inn on any given evening, which is just as well. I once sat at a round table with merchants from the farthest reaches of Sanctuary: Xiansai, Entsteig, Gea Kul . . . even a delegate from the Skovos Isles was present. Despite the disparate locations of our homes, the steaming, steep-sided platters of Bron's beef bourguignon won favor from all present. I am told this stew takes hours to create—the meat alone demands numerous steps—but I can assure you, the reward is well worth the time and effort.

Difficulty: Artisan
Prep/Cook: 4 hours, 30 minutes
Yield: 6 servings

3 pounds boneless beef chuck, cut to 1-inch cubes

1 tablespoon table salt

½ cup flour

4 tablespoons olive oil, divided

8 slices thick-cut bacon, chopped

1 medium onion, diced small

6 garlic cloves

¼ cup tomato paste

¼ cup soy sauce

1½ cups red wine

¼ cup tomato sauce or pasta sauce

3 tablespoons thyme, finely chopped

2 bay leaves

3 cups beef broth

8 ounces fresh mushrooms, quartered

5 baby carrots

12 ounces egg noodles

4 tablespoons unsalted butter, chilled

½ cup parsley, chopped

Fresh ground pepper, to taste

1. Season the beef with salt, making sure it is fully coated. Then coat the beef in flour.

2. Heat 2 tablespoons of the olive oil in a large frying pan. Fry the beef in three batches over medium-high heat until it is nicely browned on all sides. Avoid crowding the pan, which will steam the meat instead of browning it.

3. When the beef is browned, transfer it to a large casserole dish or cast-iron pot. Preheat the oven to 350°F.

4. In the same pan used for the beef, render the bacon for 2 to 3 minutes until the fat crisps and browns. Remove from the pan, and reserve the fat.

5. Add the onion, garlic, and tomato paste to the pan, and mix thoroughly for 5 minutes.

6. Add the soy sauce, red wine, and tomato sauce, and reduce by half, about 5 minutes while constantly stirring. The liquid should be a rich, dark amber.

7. Add the meat back in, along with the thyme, bay leaves, and broth. Stir well, and make sure nothing is sticking to the bottom. Cover, and reduce heat to simmer. Alternatively, you can cover the pot and place it in the oven for 3 hours at 350°F.

8. Cook for 2½ hours or until the beef is completely tender.

9. While the beef is cooking, sauté the mushrooms and carrots in 2 tablespoons of oil, and lightly season with salt, about 3 minutes.

10. When the beef has been cooking for 3 hours, add in the carrots and mushrooms, and allow the mix to cook for another 30 minutes.

Continued on the next page

TO MAKE THE NOODLES:

11. Prepare the egg noodles as desired, or based on the instructions on the package.

12. Drain, and place the warm cooked noodles in a large mixing bowl with the butter, parsley, and pepper. Coat the noodles until the butter has melted. Feel free to add a teaspoon of the cooking water to increase the heat, if needed.

13. Serve the beef in a deep plate over a bed of egg noodles.

RISING SUN COQ AU VIN

Like the pilaf, this dish has roots in Old Tristram. Othyrus based the recipe off a meal his grandfather regularly ate at the Tavern of the Rising Sun, a storied public house that once hosted infamous patrons of yore, now buried in ruins. There, locals, outlanders, heroes, and scoundrels alike gathered to tip a pint and sample the fare of the kitchen. Othyrus's grandfather learned the Rising Sun's secrets from the proprietor Ogden before misfortune befell him and this land, like so many others in Sanctuary who have met darkness unawares. Ogden's coq au vin lives on like a light in the dreary gloom.

Difficulty: Journeyman
Prep/Cook: 1 hour, 30 minutes
Yield: 4 servings

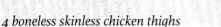

4 boneless skinless chicken thighs

4 skinned chicken legs

1 tablespoon table salt

1 teaspoon black pepper

3 tablespoons all-purpose flour

3 tablespoons extra-virgin olive oil

1 medium onion, finely chopped

1 cup leeks, thinly sliced

8 garlic cloves, thinly sliced

½ cup sherry cream

2 cups white wine

2 bay leaves

5 sprigs fresh thyme

1 pint heavy cream

1 pint cherry tomatoes, halved

4 cups baby spinach, washed

Chopped parsley for garnishing

1. Preheat the oven to 350°F.

2. Season the chicken pieces with salt and pepper, then coat them with flour.

3. In a large Dutch oven, add the olive oil; heat to medium-high.

4. Sear the chicken pieces on both sides until browned. The chicken does not need to be fully cooked. Remove chicken from the pan, and set aside.

5. In the same pan, add the onion, leeks, and garlic, and sauté over low heat for 5 to 7 minutes.

6. Add the sherry cream, and deglaze the pan, being sure to scrape the bottom bits off the pot.

7. Return the chicken to the pot; add the white wine, bay leaves, and thyme. Reduce the heat to low and simmer for 40 minutes, stirring the bottom every 10 minutes to prevent sticking.

8. Add the cream, and simmer for 10 to 15 minutes until the broth is thickened enough to coat the back of a spoon.

9. Remove from the heat, and add the halved cherry tomatoes along with the spinach. Allow the residual heat to wilt the spinach and cook the tomatoes.

10. Sprinkle with chopped parsley before serving.

COVETED GLASS NOODLES

One night, soon after the traveling caravans had closed shop, an older merchant sauntered into the bar and sat at the far end. Without a word, Bron met him with an incredible looking dish of glass noodles, the likes of which I had never seen served in the Slaughtered Calf. Envious, I asked of Bron what it took to become worthy of such service. "Shen has been a friend for many a year," he shared. Turns out that the old barkeep keeps the ingredients on-hand for this Xian favorite in case Shen rolls into town, all so that his friend can find a little bit of home on his travels. With Shen's blessing, I have collected the recipe here.

Difficulty: Journeyman
Prep/Cook: 35 minutes
Yield: 2 servings

4 cups chicken or vegetable broth

1 pinch saffron threads

8 ounces glass noodles

1 tablespoon sesame oil

1 large onion, chopped

3 garlic cloves, minced

1 cup heavy cream

Table salt, to taste

Black pepper, to taste

1 tablespoon chopped tarragon

1 tablespoon red chili paste

1. In a large saucepan, heat the broth and saffron over medium heat until simmering.

2. Soak the glass noodles in the broth for 10 to 15 minutes or until they are soft and pliable.

3. Drain the noodles, and set aside.

4. In another saucepan, heat the oil over medium heat.

5. Add the onion and garlic, and cook until soft, about 3 minutes.

6. Stir in the cream, and let the mixture come to a low simmer.

7. Add the noodles to the cream mixture, and stir until well combined. Add in a cup of the broth from the soaking noodles.

8. Season with salt and pepper, to taste.

9. Serve the pulled glass noodles in bowls, topped with the saffron broth.

10. Garnish with chopped tarragon and the chili paste.

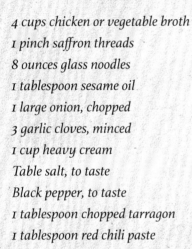

SPICED MUTTON LEG AND FLATBREAD

I have spoken to itinerant caravan traders who think of mutton as a crude food. This particular recipe obliterates that wooden belief to splinters. Its secret is the rub—a vibrant assemblage of herbs and spices that Othyrus harvests from his own garden, which he keeps well-hidden from the scavengers and wild beasts that might thieve or trample its rich flavors. The mutton meal includes a flatbread that can also serve as a trencher for a side of stew or pottage.

Difficulty: Journeyman
Prep/Cook: 4 hours
Yield: 6 servings

SPICED MUTTON LEG

2 medium onions, chopped

8 garlic cloves, minced

1-inch piece fresh ginger, grated

2 teaspoons ground cumin

2 teaspoons ground coriander

1 teaspoon ground turmeric

1 teaspoon ground cinnamon

1 teaspoon ground cardamom

2 tablespoons table salt

½ teaspoon black pepper

1 leg of lamb, about 2½ pounds

2 tablespoons vegetable oil

1 cup tomato purée

1 cup chicken broth

Fresh cilantro for garnishing

TO MAKE THE MUTTON:

1. In a large bowl, mix the onions, garlic, ginger, cumin, coriander, turmeric, cinnamon, cardamom, salt, and pepper.

2. Rub the mixture all over the leg of lamb. You can also let this sit overnight (at least 2 hours) for richer flavor.

3. In a large Dutch oven or heavy pot, heat the vegetable oil over medium-high heat.

4. Add the leg of lamb, and brown on all sides for about 5 to 7 minutes. Remove, and set aside.

5. Add the tomato purée and chicken broth, and scrape the bottom to get the fond from the pan.

6. Add the meat back in, bring to a boil, and then reduce heat to low; cover.

7. Simmer for 2 hours or until the meat is tender and falling off the bone.

8. Serve the leg of lamb with the cooking juices, garnished with cilantro and accompanied by the garlic flatbread.

Continued on the next page

FLATBREAD

3 cups all-purpose flour

1 teaspoon active dry yeast

1 teaspoon sugar

1 teaspoon table salt

½ cup warm water

¼ cup olive oil

7 garlic cloves, minced

¼ cup parsley, chopped small

TO MAKE THE FLATBREAD:

9. In a large bowl, mix the flour, yeast, sugar, and salt.

10. Gradually add the warm water and olive oil, kneading until a smooth dough forms.

11. Cover the dough, and let it rise for about 1 hour or until it has doubled in size.

12. Preheat a large skillet over medium heat.

13. Divide the dough into 4 to 6 portions.

14. Roll out each portion into a thin round shape.

15. Spread minced garlic over each dough round.

16. Cook each flatbread in the hot skillet for 2 to 3 minutes on each side or until lightly browned. Repeat until all the bread is cooked and tender.

17. Sprinkle parsley over the bread, to garnish.

18. When ready to serve, use a fork to shred the meat off the bone. Add a few ounces of meat to a piece of flatbread, and enjoy.

EIRA'S PLUM AND HONEY CAKE

Plums and honey are sweet enough to lure in any weary traveler, but when spiced with cinnamon, ginger, nutmeg, and cloves? Well, Eira tells me that she has had patrons traverse half the kingdom to feast on her plum and honey cake. I once entered the Slaughtered Calf in the early afternoon, when Eira had traded her bar rag for an apron and baked a fresh batch. Her patrons looked near to fighting for the last slice before she promised another round the following morn. This dessert disappears quickly as coin before a cutpurse.

Difficulty: Journeyman
Prep/Cook: 1 hour, 15 minutes
Yield: 8 servings

1 cup sugar

½ cup vegetable oil

2 large eggs

1 teaspoon vanilla extract

¾ cup whole milk

2 cups all-purpose flour

1 teaspoon baking powder

1 tablespoon ground cinnamon

½ teaspoon ground ginger

¼ teaspoon ground nutmeg

¼ teaspoon ground cloves

½ teaspoon table salt

8 to 10 fresh plums, pitted and sliced

8 tablespoons honey

1. Preheat oven to 350°F. Grease and flour an 8-inch round cake pan.

2. In a large mixing bowl, beat the sugar and oil together until combined. Add the eggs slowly one at a time, beating well after each addition. Stir in the vanilla extract and milk.

3. In a separate bowl, whisk together the flour, baking powder, cinnamon, ginger, nutmeg, cloves, and salt.

4. Gradually add the dry ingredients to the wet ingredients, slowly mixing until just combined.

5. Pour half of the batter into the prepared pan; using the back of a spoon, spread it evenly. Arrange half the sliced plums over the batter in a circular pattern until the base is full.

6. Spoon the remaining batter on top of the plums, and spread it evenly. Add the rest of the plums in a similar fashion on top of the cake.

7. Bake for 50 to 60 minutes or until a toothpick inserted in the center comes out somewhat clean. (If it's too clean, the cake is overbaked.)

8. Drizzle the honey over the top of the cake.

9. Let the cake cool in the pan for 10 minutes; then transfer it to a wire rack to cool completely.

ATMA'S TAVERN

LUT GHOLEIN, ARANOCH

A bustling trading port on the Twin Seas is a fine place to find seafood, and in the case of Lut Gholein, I have known this to be especially true. Bordered by Aranoch's blistering, demon-infested desert sands, this mercantile hub has proven shockingly steady against the many threats darkening its doorstep. Besides the lively markets, Lut Gholein is home to perhaps the best fish cookery in all of Sanctuary: the incomparable Atma's. The tavern hosts a plethora of surly sailors and traders, and traveling poets and local artisans, all drawn to Atma's distinct mix of maritime flavors seasoned to perfection.

I knew Atma herself to be a resilient woman whose pale ale was the stuff of legend. As she always said, "There's no trouble a mug can't cure." Over the years, she developed an arrangement with the nearby Desert Rain Inn. Its innkeeper, Elzix, would direct his hungry lodgers to Atma's for food, drink, and, depending on the clientele, entertainment. In turn, she sent them back—sated, drunk, and ready for an expensive bed. I wonder if that tradition continues . . . Atma is getting on in years, after all, and Elzix . . . well, he must be gone from this world completely by now.

For my own part, I was lucky enough to have lent my hands to Atma's kitchen over the years and to have logged her best recipes here, to share the tastes of Lut Gholein with any who think them fit.

SAND-SWEPT CEVICHE

I once made the mistake of crossing the unyielding deserts of Aranoch on foot, though I had mind enough to seek out a nomad as my guide. Even this was not without misfortune, however, as midway through the journey we found ourselves set upon by sand maggots and later trapped amid a terrible sandstorm. Hiding in the rocks of an outcropping, we waited a full day for it to die down. We kept from delving into a complete state of despair by thinking on Atma's ceviche dish, well-known to the nomad, much to my surprise. The protective boulders around us had certainly aided in our survival . . . but looking back, our primal desire for one more taste of Atma's refreshing ceviche contributed just as significantly.

Difficulty: Apprentice
Prep/Cook: 1 hour, 30 minutes
Yield: 8 servings

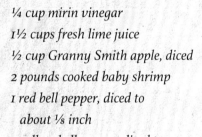

¼ cup mirin vinegar

1½ cups fresh lime juice

½ cup Granny Smith apple, diced

2 pounds cooked baby shrimp

1 red bell pepper, diced to
   about ⅛ inch

1 yellow bell pepper, diced to
   about ⅛ inch

1 whole serrano pepper, seeded
   and vein removed, minced

½ cup shallot, finely chopped

2 tablespoons red chili paste
   or sriracha

Kosher salt, to taste

Black pepper, to taste

1 ripe avocado, pitted and
   diced small

½ cup fresh chives

Tortilla chips for serving

1 lime, cut into quarters,
   for serving

1. In a small bowl, add mirin vinegar, lime juice, and diced apples. Set aside, to avoid browning.

2. In a large bowl, add the shrimp, bell peppers, serrano pepper, shallot, and red chili paste, and mix until fully incorporated. Season with salt and pepper.

3. Add in the avocado and the mirin mix, and gently mix with a spoon. Be careful to not overmix or mash the avocado; it should be gently blended.

4. Place in the refrigerator, and marinate for 10 to 20 minutes (or a maximum of 1 hour).

5. Place in a serving bowl, and sprinkle chives on top.

6. Serve with a side of tortilla chips and limes.

CORSAIR SHAKSHUKA AND CRUSTY BREAD

Precious few corners of Sanctuary are free from the threat of piracy, and Lut Gholein is no exception. The sails that one sees down by the docks are dyed blue to evade corsairs and improve a vessel's chances of reaching port unharmed. This poached-egg fare is popular amongst those ships' sailors, who must face the perils of the Twin Seas and beyond. It is fairly simple to make: Pressing a spoon into the sauce, and then cracking the eggs gently into the wells is the most challenging part, and far less challenging than facing down pirates.

Difficulty: Apprentice
Prep/Cook: 35 minutes
Yield: 4 servings

CRUSTY BREAD

*1 loaf hard-crust bread
  (ciabatta, focaccia, or a baguette)*
1 garlic clove
3 tablespoons olive oil
Table salt, to taste
Black pepper, to taste

SHAKSHUKA

1 tablespoon olive oil
*1 medium yellow onion,
  sliced about ⅛ inch thin*
3 large plum tomatoes, diced large
6 garlic cloves, sliced thin
1½ cups canned tomato sauce
*3 tablespoons smoked paprika,
  plus extra for garnishing*
1 tablespoon ground cumin
2 tablespoons capers
1 tablespoon red chili flakes
5 whole eggs
¼ bunch parsley, chopped

TO MAKE THE CRUSTY BREAD:

1. Preheat the oven to 375°F.

2. Slice the bread to ½ inch thick, to make three easy-to-handle slices.

3. Gently rub 1 garlic clove on each piece of bread, on both sides. This gives a subtle garlic flavor. Alternatively, you can mince the garlic and spread it evenly across the bread.

4. Drizzle olive oil on top of the bread; use your fingers to spread it evenly on both sides of the toast. Then sprinkle with salt and pepper.

5. On a baking sheet, lay the bread flat, and bake for 8 minutes on one side; then flip each piece over, and bake for another 12 minutes until brown.

TO MAKE THE SHAKSHUKA:

6. Heat a large cast-iron skillet over medium-high heat.

7. Add the oil, onion, diced tomato, and garlic, and sauté until the tomato is slightly softened. Add in the tomato sauce, and stir.

8. Turn down the heat to medium-low, and continue to stir until reduced and thickened by half, about 5 minutes. The mix should be thick and a bit chunky.

9. Add in the paprika, cumin, capers, and chili flakes, and stir thoroughly.

10. Using the back of a spoon, make small wells in a circle around the edge of the pan.

11. Crack your eggs into a separate small bowl or ramekin, and gently place 1 egg in each well.

12. Place in the oven, and bake for 3 to 5 minutes for runny eggs, 6 to 8 minutes for hard yolks.

13. Remove the pan from the oven, and then sprinkle with paprika and parsley.

14. Serve with crusty bread.

ARANOCH BAY SCALLOPS WITH TARRAGON CREAM SAUCE

Difficulty: Artisan
Prep/Cook: 45 minutes
Yield: 4 servings

As the primary trade conduit for the Western Kingdoms, Lut Gholein sees a diverse stream of folk flowing through its marketplaces and into its taverns. At Atma's, I had noted that many visitors, regardless of origin or destination, would order a plate of these golden, caramelized scallops drizzled with a lightly simmered tarragon cream sauce.

2 pounds bay scallops

4 tablespoons unsalted butter, divided

2 tablespoons olive oil

2 garlic cloves

Table salt, to taste

Black pepper, to taste

1 shallot, chopped

½ tablespoon cornstarch

½ cup dry white wine

1 cup seafood or chicken broth

1 cup heavy cream

2 tablespoons fresh tarragon, finely chopped

1. Rinse the bay scallops under cold running water, and pat dry with paper towels.

2. Heat the butter and olive oil in a large skillet over medium heat.

3. Add the garlic, and cook for about 30 seconds until fragrant.

4. Season with salt and pepper, then add the scallops to the skillet.

5. Cook the scallops for 2 to 3 minutes on each side until they are golden brown and opaque.

6. When the scallops are golden and caramelized, remove them to a plate.

7. Add 1 tablespoon butter to the pan, and melt at low heat.

8. Add the chopped shallots. Stirring constantly, cook for 3 minutes until they have softened.

9. Add the cornstarch, and stir until all the granules have vanished.

10. Pour the white wine into the pan, and let it simmer for 2 minutes until it has reduced slightly. Use a wooden spoon to stir the mixture and to lift any caramelized bits from the pan.

11. Pour in the broth and cream, and add the fresh tarragon.

12. Let the sauce simmer gently for a few minutes, constantly stirring, until you have a thick consistency that coats the back of a spoon.

13. Taste for seasoning, and then add the scallops back in. Coat with the sauce and serve.

PORT TOWN POTATO-CRUSTED COD

It was a blustery day at the tail end of a nasty sandstorm when I first tried this dish. After I passed several of Lut Gholein's stalls in the swirling grit, squinting through my scarf, I ducked into Atma's for a bite. I was shaking a layer of sand off my cloak at the bar while Atma greeted me: "Tedric, you look like a crusted cod." I said that I certainly felt like one. She said, "Well then, I have the perfect plate for you." And she certainly did: this potato-crusted cod. Needless to say, I cajoled the recipe from her before I even finished the meal.

Difficulty: Artisan
Prep/Cook: 1 hour, 30 minutes
Yield: 4 servings

PUMPKIN SEED PESTO

1 poblano pepper, seeded and chopped

½ cup roasted pumpkin seeds

½ cup olive oil

6 garlic cloves

2 tablespoons table salt

1 cup basil

POTATO-CRUSTED COD

1 cup all-purpose flour

3 eggs

1 cup mashed potato flakes

½ teaspoon table salt

⅛ teaspoon black pepper

1 teaspoon garlic powder

1 teaspoon onion powder

1 teaspoon dried parsley

Four 4-ounce cod fillets

¼ cup canola oil

1 medium lemon, halved

TO MAKE THE PESTO:

1. In a food processor, add the pepper, pumpkin seeds, olive oil, and garlic, and pulse 4 to 6 times until chopped.

2. Then add the salt and basil, and blend until the mix is chunky. Avoid overmixing or turning the mix smooth. Set aside.

TO MAKE THE COD:

3. Add the flour to a shallow bowl. In a second bowl, whisk together the eggs. In a third bowl, combine the potato flakes, salt, pepper, garlic powder, onion powder, and parsley.

4. Dredge the cod fillets in the flour, shaking off the excess. Then dip each fillet into the eggs until coated, letting the excess drip off.

5. Coat each fillet with the potato flakes mixture, and set on a clean plate.

6. Heat the oil in a deep skillet over medium heat.

7. Add the cod fillets to the skillet, and cook for 3 to 4 minutes per side until golden brown. Go slow here until the fish is cooked through and the internal temperature reaches 145°F.

8. Transfer the fillets to a paper towel–lined plate before serving, to absorb excess oil.

9. Top the fish with 1 tablespoon of pesto, and then squeeze the fresh lemon over the top.

KHAZRA CARROTS

In a port filled with all the wondrous victuals of Sanctuary, it always surprised me that this simple sliced carrot dish remained a cornerstone of Atma's offerings. She noted that, particularly in times of hardship, root vegetables were the one consistency amid the ever-changing landscape of the marketplace. Elzix put it best when he stumbled upon guests, stuffing their gullets with these tasty, charred slivers: "Not even goatmen enjoy carrots this much."

Difficulty: Apprentice
Prep/Cook: 45 minutes
Yield: 4 servings

1 pound carrots (peeled, trimmed, and cut into ¼-inch thick slices) on the bias

1 teaspoon tomato paste

3 tablespoons olive oil

1 teaspoon cumin

1 tablespoon paprika

½ teaspoon lemon pepper

1 cup Parmesan cheese, shredded

Fresh chives to garnish

1. Preheat oven to 425° F.

2. Mix the cumin, paprika, and lemon pepper with the oil and tomato paste.

3. Coat the carrots with the rub and then dip them in the Parmesan, coating them evenly.

4. Roast the carrots for 15 minutes and then flip them. Roast for another 15 minutes or until carrots are charred and fork-tender.

5. Remove from the oven and garnish with chives.

TWIN SEAS SEAFOOD STEW

Though the stalls of Lut Gholein's markets seldom open before sunrise, I knew Atma to procure her essentials before the day's wares could be unloaded from its ships. She would haggle with the fishmongers for their freshest wares or make straight for the docks in hopes of building upon her menu for a fairer price. This extraordinary seafood stew takes its flavor from shrimp; mussels; cod; a soup base of chorizo, onion, and tomatoes with white wine; and, crucially, the perfect assortment of garden herbs. Serve it with a generous chunk of the aforementioned crusty bread for a complete meal.

Difficulty: Artisan
Prep/Cook: 45 minutes
Yield: 4 servings

---

2 tablespoons canola oil

8 ounces Mexican chorizo, removed from casing (alternatively, you can use spicy Italian sausage)

1 small yellow onion, chopped small

5 garlic cloves, sliced thin

1 tablespoon tomato paste

2 tablespoons flour

1 tablespoon dry oregano

1 tablespoon dry basil

¼ cup white wine

2 cups clam juice

Two 14.5-ounce cans diced tomatoes

1½ pounds large wild shrimp, peeled, deveined, and tails removed

½ bag mussels, cleaned

½ pound cod or tilapia, diced into ¼-inch pieces

1 bunch fresh cilantro, chopped

4 tablespoons unsalted butter

1 medium lemon, sliced

1 tablespoon extra-virgin olive oil, for garnish

Table salt, to taste

Black pepper, to taste

1. In a large soup or stock pot, add the oil and chorizo. You can also do this in a wok.

2. Using a wooden spoon, cook the chorizo over medium heat until slightly browned, being sure to break up any chunks; sauté about 4 to 5 minutes or until the chunks have slightly crisped up.

3. Add the onions and garlic and sauté until fragrant, about 1 minute.

4. Add the tomato paste, flour, oregano, and basil, and continue cooking for 2 more minutes, making sure all the flour is mixed.

5. Add the white wine, and deglaze the pan, being sure to scrape the bottom. The mixture will look slightly thickened.

6. Add the clam juice and diced tomatoes, and bring back to a low boil. Be sure to taste the liquid; the mixture should be slightly saltier than desired because it will reduce in intensity when you add the seafood.

7. Add the shrimp, mussels, and cod into the soup, and gently mix until coated, being careful not to break up the fish.

8. Cover with a lid, and cook until the mussels have opened, about 5 to 8 minutes. If any fail to open, discard them because they are bad and not safe to eat.

9. Remove the lid, and turn off the heat.

10. Add the cilantro (reserving a small amount for garnish) and butter, and mix until the butter is melted.

11. Pour into large bowls, with an additional small bowl on hand for the discarded mussel shells.

12. Garnish with a lemon slice, cilantro, a drizzle of olive oil and salt and pepper to taste, and serve with crusty bread (page 41).

MARAUDER'S ORANGE SPICE CAKE

Atma related to me the origin of this recipe, one of the more interesting tales I have ever heard. A patron sent her way by Elzix came to the inn—he could not afford room and board at the Desert Rain and needed a day's wages. As proof of his skill in the kitchen, he offered her a bite of this cake. If she liked it, he would give her the recipe and his ready hands in exchange for coin. She enjoyed it so much, she gave him work for the better part of a fortnight . . . until he drew in a band of brigands who nearly tore the place apart to find him. Perhaps this recipe is all that remains of the poor man.

Difficulty: Journeyman
Prep/Cook: 1 hour, 15 minutes
Yield: 8 to 10 servings

SPICE CAKE

2½ cups all-purpose flour

2 teaspoons double-acting baking powder

1 teaspoon baking soda

½ teaspoon table salt

2 teaspoons ground cinnamon

1 teaspoon ground ginger

1 teaspoon ground nutmeg

1 teaspoon ground allspice

½ cup granulated sugar

½ cup light brown sugar

¾ cup vegetable oil

3 large eggs

1 teaspoon almond extract

1 cup freshly squeezed orange juice

½ cup chopped walnuts

2 cups shredded carrots

Zest from orange (blood orange is best)

ORANGE GLAZE

1 cup powdered sugar

2 tablespoons freshly squeezed orange juice

1 teaspoon grated ginger

1 tablespoon unsalted butter, melted

TO MAKE THE CAKE:

1. Preheat the oven to 350°F. Grease a 9-by-13-inch cake pan.

2. In a medium bowl, whisk together the flour, baking powder, baking soda, salt, cinnamon, ginger, nutmeg, and allspice.

3. In a large bowl, beat together granulated sugar, brown sugar, oil, eggs, and almond extract until smooth. Gradually add in the flour mixture and the orange juice, alternating until just combined. Fold in the chopped walnuts and carrots.

4. Pour the batter into the prepared pan and top with orange zest.

5. Bake for 45 to 50 minutes or until a toothpick inserted into the center comes out clean. Let cool completely. The cake should be thick and dense.

TO MAKE THE GLAZE:

6. Whisk together the powdered sugar, orange juice, ginger, and melted butter until smooth. Drizzle the glaze over the cooled cake, and serve.

THE CAPTAIN'S TABLE

GEA KUL, KEHJISTAN

Some say Kehjistan, once the mainstay of civilization and trade in Sanctuary, now produces more scorpions than art or commerce. But last I knew, travelers slogging through the demons and cultists of the Borderlands could still find respite in the crumbling port town of Gea Kul. There, over a river and down a muddy lane lined with tumbledown shanties, was a place known as the Captain's Table.

My mother did a stint at the Captain's Table when I was just a boy, barely the height of the bar. I remember Gea Kul to be terrifying, but back then the inn's legendary founder, Captain Hanos Jeronnan, showed me kindness after unlocking the bolt on the door and letting me into an empty dining room. If the bolt had not told me everything I needed to know, the boards nailed across the windows did.

The captain was a formidable man with stark, snow-white hair and a deep, garrulous voice. Apparently, he had named his inn after a term used in the Westmarch navy for the quarterly meetings held with other captains. He also ensured his inn was scrubbed top to bottom with salt water and vinegar—an old trick for keeping ships clean.

Folks would travel far to devour Captain Jeronnan's celebrated cheesy hand pie or a plate of his spiced shortbread cookies. I was particularly fond of the glowing hearth in the place. A crackling communal fireplace may seem an odd feature for an inn situated just south of Kehjistan's blazing dunes, but as those who traverse the searing sands well know, the high desert packs a frigid bite once the sun slips below the horizon.

I heard the captain met his end some years ago, when he stepped in to help a poor innocent whom some brigand was shaking down for coin, and got stabbed for his troubles. Phorar, his former cabin boy, took over running the public house in memory of his lost captain. Since Phorar has never written to this old traveler, I was thrilled to discover that he had kept Captain Jeronnan's recipes alive.

CHEESY HAND PIE

If ever one were to get lost in the disorienting intersections of the city, the mouthwatering smell of this cheesy hand pie would lead them right to the door of the Captain's Table. Shortly after I consumed one of these hand pies, I became an intolerable nuisance, pestering the staff until they let me in on the recipe. Since that day, the aroma of seared halloumi cheese makes me drool like a ravenous wolf—especially when it is coming from my own oven.

Difficulty: Artisan
Prep/Cook: 50 minutes
Yield: 5 to 6 servings

1 tablespoon vegetable oil

1 small onion, chopped
  (about ¼ cup)

2 garlic cloves, minced

½ pound halloumi cheese, chopped
  into small cubes (alternatively,
  you can use queso fresco cheese)

1 egg

2 tablespoons all-purpose flour

1 package puff pastry sheets,
  thawed

½ teaspoon table salt

1. Heat the oil in a 10-inch skillet over medium-high heat.

2. Add the onion and garlic, and cook for 2 minutes, stirring occasionally.

3. Add the halloumi cheese, and sear one side until slightly brown; then remove from the pan. Set this mix aside. If using other cheese, skip this step.

4. Preheat the oven to 400°F.

5. Line a baking sheet with parchment paper.

6. In a small bowl, beat the egg with a fork, and set aside.

7. Sprinkle the flour on your work surface. Unfold 1 pastry sheet.

8. Roll the pastry sheet into a 1 foot square.

9. Using a round cutter, cut the pastry into four 5-inch circles. Repeat with the remaining pastry sheet.

10. Spoon about 2 tablespoons of the cheese mixture into the center of each pastry circle. Fold the pastry over the filling, and press the edges to seal. Crimp the edges with a fork.

11. Using a sharp knife, cut small slits in the tops of the pastries. Then place the pastries onto the baking sheet.

12. Brush the pastries with the egg wash, and sprinkle with salt.

13. Place in the oven, and bake for 15 minutes or until the pastries are golden brown. Let the pastries cool on the baking sheet on a wire rack for 10 minutes.

LAUDED LAMINATED PANCAKES

I have many fond memories of these pancakes sizzling over a hot griddle and my mother would let me sneak a taste before a fresh batch made its way out of the kitchen. At the Captain's Table, I watched many a hardened warrior, spurning the idea of sweets in the morning, but regretting the words when these pancakes reached their table. The preparation requires a keen attention to detail. It is essential to smooth each dough ball, making sure the texture is elastic, not sticky. The folding of the cakes is quite a delicate undertaking as well, but well worth a fine breakfast to start the day.

Difficulty: Master
Prep/Cook: 2 hours
Yield: 10 to 12 pancakes

3½ cups all-purpose flour,
  plus more as needed

½ cup fine semolina

2 teaspoons sugar

2 teaspoons kosher salt

¼ teaspoon active dry yeast

1½ cups warm water, plus
  more as needed

1½ cups vegetable oil

½ cup unsalted butter, melted

¾ cup salted butter, room
  temperature, divided

1 cup strawberry jam

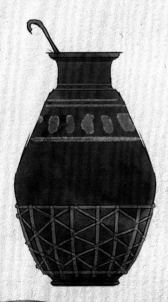

1. Mix the flour, semolina, sugar, salt, and yeast in a large bowl. Add the water, and combine to make a dough.

2. Knead the dough by hand (or with a mixer and dough hook) until very smooth, soft, and elastic, but not sticky. Adjust the water or flour as necessary to achieve that texture.

3. Divide the dough into balls about the size of a lime. Be sure the top and sides of the balls are smooth. Transfer the balls of dough onto an oiled tray or plate, cover loosely with plastic, and leave to rest for 20 minutes.

4. Place each bowl of butter and oil to the side of your flat workstation, and prepare to press the dough.

5. Add a small amount of oil (about 1 teaspoon) to your work surface, and place a single ball of dough on it.

6. Using your hands, flatten the dough as thin as you can—almost thin enough to see through, but without tearing.

7. Using a pastry brush, coat the surface of the dough with butter and sprinkle with salt; fold the dough in half, and repeat. Do this until you have folded four to six times. It should be folded enough that it neatly fits into your frying pan or griddle surface. Repeat this process with the remaining balls of dough. You can store these for up to 48 hours in the refrigerator.

8. Place a heavy-bottomed skillet over medium heat, or use a griddle set to 350°F.

9. Flatten your dough one last time so that it is just large enough to be a square inside the pan, about 4 to 5 inches in size.

10. Cook the bread, flipping every 2 minutes until both sides are a deep golden brown (about 8 to 10 minutes per piece of dough).

11. When the dough is cooked, remove and place on a plate. Using a spoon, brush the top of the dough with ½ tablespoon room temperature butter. Repeat with the remaining dough.

12. Serve with the strawberry jam on the side.

SIGHTLESS EYE AHI TUNA

One evening, I was delighted to find myself seated next to an Askari sailor. Over the course of several hours, she would regale me with tales from her homeland—so many that I could fill an entirely new tome with her stories alone. However, the story that captured my imagination the most was that of the Sightless Eye. This artifact supposedly allows its wielder not only to communicate across vast distances, but also to glimpse into their future. As dinner was served, I couldn't help wondering if the fresh ahi tuna on my plate would have appreciated use of the Sightless Eye, if for nothing more than to avoid fishing nets.

Difficulty: Journeyman
Prep/Cook: 35 minutes
Yield: 12 to 14 bites

PARMESAN CRISPS
½ cup grated Parmesan cheese

TUNA
3 tablespoons white sesame seeds
3 tablespoons black sesame seeds
1 teaspoon sugar
2 tablespoons soy sauce or
   liquid aminos
1 pound ahi tuna, fresh or thawed
2 tablespoons vegetable or
   grapeseed oil
1 teaspoon sesame oil
1 tablespoon sea salt

TO MAKE THE PARMESAN CRISPS:

1. Preheat oven to 400°F.

2. Pour a large spoonful of cheese onto a parchment-lined baking sheet, and gently flatten the cheese with the bottom of the spoon.

3. Fill the tray with cheese mounds, keeping them about ½ inch apart from one another. Place in the oven, and bake for 5 to 8 minutes or until the cheese is golden brown.

4. Allow to cool for 5 minutes. Then carefully remove the crisps from the tray, and cool for an additional 5 minutes.

TO MAKE THE TUNA:

5. Place the black and white sesame seeds and sugar in a medium bowl or plate. Pour the soy sauce into a deep bowl or a flat plate.

6. Pat dry the ahi tuna with paper towels. Place the tuna on a plate, and coat all sides with soy sauce.

7. Dip the tuna into the sesame mix while generously sprinkling all sides of the ahi tuna with additional sesame mix, pressing it down into the flesh and coating as much as possible.

8. Heat a heavy skillet or frying pan to high heat. Add the vegetable oil and sesame oil to the pan.

9. Carefully place the coated tuna on the pan, and sear for 60 seconds or until the white sesame seeds are golden brown. Be careful to watch for burning.

10. Turn the tuna until all sides are properly seared. Remove from the pan, and let rest for 2 minutes.

11. Gently slice each piece of tuna into a ¼-inch slice. Place a tuna slice on each Parmesan crisp, and sprinkle with sea salt.

CAPTAIN'S CREW FISH STEW

I fondly recall one riotous evening when a group of forty or so sailors filled the tavern, such that we turned away many a patron. The party was loud and boisterous, and a strange, steely look came over the captain upon seeing them. He told my mother to step aside, for he knew what had brought them here. As my mother and I rushed from table to bar, filling mugs and clearing tables, an awed silence settled over the inn. I turned to see the captain lugging over a steaming, fragrant cauldron of this fish stew—the captain's most cherished recipe—meant to feed the crew of an entire ship. For these sailors were once the captain's own, and they made a pilgrimage to his table any time they made port in Gea Kul. I eagerly helped the captain ladle up and then refill their bowls, and some of the sailors spilled them in their inebriation, laughing about the tragedy of wasting a single drop. In no time, we were scraping the deep bottom of the cauldron, and the crew stumbled off into the night. I remember well the sad sort of smile on the captain's face as he watched them go.

Difficulty: Journeyman
Prep/Cook: 1 hour, 30 minutes
Yield: 4 servings

2 tablespoons extra-virgin olive oil

1 medium red onion, diced

2 large celery stalks, diced

2 medium carrots, diced

1 medium zucchini, diced

2 to 3 garlic cloves, minced

Sea salt, to taste

Black pepper, to taste

½ cup dry white wine

One 28-ounce can chopped tomatoes, with liquid

4 cups fish stock

1 pound halibut fillets, with skin removed and roughly chopped

1 cup fresh green beans, trimmed and quartered

1 large lemon, juiced and zested

¾ cup fresh parsley, chopped

¼ cup pine nuts

1. Heat the olive oil in a large soup pot over medium heat.

2. Add the onion, celery, carrots, zucchini, and garlic to the pot.

3. Season the vegetables with salt and pepper to taste.

4. Cook the vegetables, stirring occasionally, until they become soft and fragrant, around 4 to 5 minutes.

5. Pour the wine into the pot, and use a wooden spoon to scrape any brown bits off the bottom.

6. Stir to combine, and simmer for 2 to 3 minutes.

7. Add the chopped tomatoes and fish stock to the pot, and bring to a rapid boil.

8. Reduce heat to medium-low, cover the pot, and gently simmer (stirring occasionally) for 20 to 25 minutes.

9. Uncover the pot, and add the chopped halibut and fresh green beans.

10. Cover, and continue cooking until the fish is flaky and the green beans are slightly tender, around 8 to 10 minutes.

11. Stir in the lemon juice, lemon zest, pine nuts, and fresh parsley.

12. Remove from heat, and season with additional salt and pepper.

NECROMANCER'S BROILED FISH

Difficulty: Artisan
Prep/Cook: 1 hour
Yield: 2 servings

The last time I feasted on this marvelous dish, a rasping, decrepit old gaffer slid in next to me, sloshing a mug of ale. With a gap-toothed grin, he launched into a tale from half a century past. It was a cold night, he recalled, and he sat at this very bar, trying (and failing) to quench his considerable thirst for solace. Suddenly, a loud burst of zeal from sailors in a nearby booth drew his attention. He followed their eager gaze to the entrance, where a young lady with striking silver eyes and raven hair had just stepped inside. Clearly travel-worn and troubled, the woman silenced the rowdy deckhands with a single icy glance. (Later, the man learned it was Kara Nightshadow, a Rathma necromancer of some note.) Keen-eyed Captain Jeronnan hurried to attend, serving her cider and his signature plate, the broiled fish. The restorative effect was marked and immediate.

½ cup melted unsalted butter

¼ cup lemon juice

¼ cup soy sauce

1½ pounds tilapia

1 teaspoon garlic powder
  (or 2 garlic cloves, minced)

1 tablespoon paprika

Table salt, to taste

Black pepper, to taste

1. Preheat the broiler; if you don't have a broiler, preheat the oven to 450°F.

2. In a bowl, mix the melted butter, lemon juice, and soy sauce.

3. Season both sides of the tilapia fillets with garlic powder, paprika, salt, and pepper.

4. Grease a baking dish, and arrange the seasoned tilapia fillets in the dish.

5. Pour the butter, lemon juice, and soy sauce mixture over the tilapia fillets.

6. Broil in the preheated oven for 6 to 8 minutes or until the tilapia is cooked through and the top is lightly browned, with an internal temperature of 145°F. If roasting, bake for 15 to 20 minutes.

HOODWINKED HONEY CARROTS

The captain had borrowed this recipe from a feast hall that catered to the gentry. As my mother ladled it onto my pewter dish, she spoke to the captain's unmatched affinity for honey sticks. Apparently, a pair of hapless swindlers sat bickering in a booth one night. Among other dishes, they had consumed substantial helpings of finely cured meats and these honey-roasted carrots, plus several strong brews. One staggered to the entrance then turned to blurt a final insult. The other seized cutlery and gave chase. It had all been a ruse—a feeble attempt to dine without paying—but as they fled to the doorway, they ran into Captain Jeronnan. One look at the rare upset on the proprietor's face stopped them in their tracks. The brigands spent the next three hours scouring pots at his washing basin . . . but the kindly captain still treated them to honey sticks as they sobered up.

Difficulty: Apprentice
Prep/Cook: 35 minutes
Yield: 6 servings

---

2 pounds carrots, peeled and
   ends trimmed

2 tablespoons olive oil

2 garlic cloves, minced

¾ teaspoon table salt, plus more
   as desired

½ teaspoon black pepper

3 tablespoons honey

¼ bunch parsley, chopped

1. Preheat oven to 430°F.

2. Cut the carrots on the bias into 2-inch-long pieces. Cut the thicker ones in half lengthwise so they are all roughly the same size. (You can also use farm-fresh carrots and cut them in half lengthwise for a nicer presentation.)

3. Place the carrots in a large bowl; then drizzle with oil, add in the garlic, sprinkle with salt and pepper, and toss together.

4. On a baking tray, lay the carrots flat. Drizzle the honey evenly on top.

5. Roast for 10 minutes or until the carrots start to char and get some color.

6. Remove from the oven, and flip over the carrots to cook for another 10 minutes or until fork-tender.

7. Sprinkle with parsley, and season with salt once more to taste.

RESHOMI'S SPICED SHORTBREAD

This treat facilitated a great friendship. In the ignorance of my youth, I complained to the captain that—besides his much beloved honey sticks—he had scarcely any sweets among his offerings. Some weeks later, a platter of this shortbread arrived in the hands of a woman wearing a red hooded cloak. Her name was Reshomi and, as it turns out, she baked for a great noble in Caldeum. The captain had written to her and offered payment in exchange for the secrets of her trade: puddings and tarts, and marzipan cakes and heavy creams. I became her shadow in the kitchen, finding her every confection a wonder, although I must confess, I retain a soft spot for the very first dish of hers I sampled—her spiced shortbread.

Difficulty: Journeyman
Prep/Cook: 45 minutes
Yield: 12 to 14 cookies

1 cup unsalted butter, room temperature

⅔ cup sugar

½ teaspoon almond extract

2 cups all-purpose flour

1 teaspoon cinnamon

⅛ teaspoon nutmeg

½ cup raspberry jam

1. Combine butter, sugar, and almond extract in a medium mixing bowl.

2. Mix at medium speed, scraping the bowl often, until creamy.

3. Reduce speed, and add in flour, cinnamon, and nutmeg. Beat until well mixed, about 3 minutes.

4. Keep beating until the dough starts to come together. It will look somewhat dry and crumbly at first, but it will come together in time.

5. Remove the dough from the mixer, form it into a ball, and cover. Refrigerate until firm, at least 2 hours.

6. Preheat the oven to 350°F.

7. Remove the dough from the refrigerator, and place it on your work surface.

8. Shape dough into 1-inch balls.

9. Place dough balls 2 inches apart on an ungreased cookie sheet.

10. Make an indentation with your thumb in the center of each ball.

11. Fill each indentation with ¼ teaspoon jam. Be careful to not overfill.

12. Bake for 14 minutes or until the edges are lightly browned.

13. Let the cookies stand 1 minute, remove from cookie sheet, and cool completely before serving.

WOLF CITY TAVERN

CITY OF WESTMARCH, WESTMARCH

As a renowned river port and berth of the Westmarch Navy, this capital city hosts quite a wide-ranging assortment of visitors and refugees, both highborn and lowborn. Trekking across the outer wards, a hungry wanderer may stumble upon Wolf City Tavern and mistake it for merely another nondescript watering hole. Although it squats in Gideon's Row—a district of low repute, often ignored by the Westmarch Guard patrols—this remarkable venue is great comfort against a dark and foreboding night. Here, one can cozy up to the bar, order a mulled red wine, and purchase some of the finest tavern fare this side of the Twin Seas.

I was barely a young man during my stint there, still traveling with my mother as I learned her trade. I knew the bartender, Bailey, was oft involved with mysterious deeds of some sort—always taking meetings with folk in hushed tones. Whatever else he was involved in, he ran a tight kitchen, and his dealings never negatively affected the quality of the food or vintage. Enclosed are a few of the foodstuffs that I poached from this traveler's haven; of particular note are the crab salad buns and the venison stew.

BANDIT'S BACON CANDY

It has been said that this treat is good enough to risk life and limb to filch. I first sampled it years ago at a Lunasadh harvest festival—a somewhat subdued affair even in its heyday, with a crop of tattered tents sprouting from the hamlets outside the capital's gates. Bailey and I were preoccupied serving the tavern's spiced bacon candy to the locals swarming his booth when a man cut the line and made off with an entire platter. Bailey said the man resurfaced three days later, strung up along the Justinian road near the Wolf Gate, likely having stolen something of greater value than our confections.

Difficulty: Journeyman
Prep/Cook: 1 hour, 15 minutes
Yield: 10 to 12 pieces

1 pound thick-cut bacon
½ cup brown sugar
½ teaspoon cracked black pepper
¼ teaspoon cayenne pepper
½ tablespoon red pepper flakes

1. Preheat oven to 375°F.

2. Line a baking sheet pan with a silicone liner, parchment paper, aluminum foil, or a wire rack.

3. Lay bacon onto the tray until the sheet pan is full, but do not overlap slices.

4. In a small bowl, add brown sugar, black pepper, cayenne pepper, and red pepper flakes. Stir to combine.

5. Sprinkle the mixture over the top of the slices and pat it down gently.

6. Bake until brown and crispy or up to 40 minutes.

7. Remove from the oven and allow to cool for 15 to 20 minutes.

8. Cut in half, then serve.

ESSEN'S SPIT-ROASTED PORK

Though my mother's skill did much to elevate Wolf City Tavern above its competition, she had little experience cooking highborn delicacies. After all, most inns can only afford the most basic ingredients. Wolf City Tavern's patrons, however, were not limited to the common folk, so Bailey brought on not one but two exemplary cooks, Essen and Wessel, from the manors of wealthy lords in Westmarch. Oddly enough, they also came bearing sacks of seasonings from their lords' expansive spiceries. (Bailey may have extorted them for their service and resources; nobody knew for sure or would have dared accuse him.) Regardless, this spit-roasted pork became quite the favorite, and Essen trained my mother in its preparation. When their time with Wolf City Tavern was over, my mother continued to offer it . . . at least, until the spices ran out.

Difficulty: Journeyman
Prep/Cook: 1 hour
Yield: 4 servings

PORK

2 tablespoons olive oil
1 tablespoon dried thyme
1 tablespoon dried rosemary
1½ tablespoons paprika
1 tablespoon garlic powder
2 tablespoons table salt
3⅓ pounds pork loin, diced
   into ½-inch cubes
2 red bell peppers, diced
   into ½-inch pieces
2 green bell peppers, diced
   into ½-inch pieces

LEMON HONEY SAUCE

¼ cup lemon juice
½ cup honey
2 garlic cloves, minced
½ teaspoon table salt
1 teaspoon black pepper
½ teaspoon Tabasco or hot sauce

TO MAKE THE PORK:

1. In a small bowl, mix the olive oil, thyme, rosemary, paprika, garlic powder, and salt.

2. Brush the seasoned oil all over the pork cubes and bell peppers.

3. Alternately, thread the pork cubes and peppers onto wooden skewers.

4. Place the skewers on a rotisserie or a spit, if using a grill. If using a grill, you can also place the excess peppers in a foil pouch next to the skewers.

5. Cook the pork over an open flame or on the grill, turning it periodically, for about 20 minutes or until the internal temperature reaches 160°F.

TO MAKE THE SAUCE:

6. In a small saucepan, mix the lemon juice, honey, garlic, salt, pepper, and Tabasco sauce.

7. Heat the sauce over medium heat, stirring occasionally, until well combined and slightly thickened.

8. Brush the sauce over the pork and peppers during the last 5 minutes of cooking.

9. Serve the pork hot, garnished with additional sauce, if desired.

WOLF CITY WATERMELON AND SPINACH SALAD

Difficulty: Apprentice
Prep/Cook: 20 minutes
Yield: 6 to 8 servings

In bygone times, before the strange siege of death that befell Westmarch (and swept over much of Sanctuary itself), Wolf City Tavern was rife with song. I often think on this era, of shyly asking the barmaid to first dance with me during a slow night. I suppose the serving staff and regular patrons—perhaps that barmaid too—are long dead by now. Having seen horrible atrocities in life, it reminds me of the delight we must take when we can. Tomorrow is not promised, after all, and the forces at play in our world are beyond any of our understanding. Today, I celebrate the memory of those lively evenings with this refreshing starter dish from their offerings.

DRESSING

½ cup white balsamic vinegar

3 tablespoons flavorless oil, such as avocado or safflower oil

1 tablespoon poppy seeds

2 tablespoons maple syrup

1 teaspoon Dijon mustard

1 teaspoon kosher salt

SALAD

8 cups baby spinach, shredded paper thin

3 cups watermelon, seedless, diced about 1 inch thick

1½ cups goat cheese

¼ cup toasted pumpkin seeds

1. Prepare the dressing by whisking or blending the vinegar, oil, poppy seeds, maple syrup, mustard, and salt.

2. Rinse and dry the baby spinach.

3. Tightly roll a handful of leaves together to form a cigar shape.

4. Very thinly slice or chiffonade the roll of spinach; repeat until all the spinach has been shredded. Set aside.

5. Place the watermelon in a medium or large bowl. Coat the watermelon in the dressing, and check for taste.

6. Add in the shredded spinach, and gently mix until coated.

7. To serve, place a bed of the spinach-and-watermelon mix on a large, flat plate.

8. Sprinkle the goat cheese on top of the spinach-and-watermelon mix. Try to avoid large clumps.

9. Season once more with salt, and then garnish with the toasted pumpkin seeds.

LONGSHOREMAN'S CRAB SALAD BUNS

Long has animosity festered between Westmarch's sailors and longshoremen. The sailors think the longshoremen inferior for their unwillingness to go to sea, while the longshoremen resent the sailors for their brief, riotous tours through the city. Many a tavern has seen this conflict come to blows, but very seldom at Wolf City. Bailey kept both groups stuffed to the gills with the tavern's specialty: this salad of diced onion, cucumber, chives, and crab meat served up in a warm bun. Its incredible flavor may be the one thing on which these two trades have ever agreed.

Difficulty: Apprentice
Prep/Cook: 4 hours, 30 minutes
Yield: 8 to 10 sandwiches

CRAB SALAD

1 pound lump crab meat
¼ cup red onion, diced small
¼ cup cucumber, diced small
4 tablespoons chopped chives
½ cup mayonnaise
1 tablespoon Dijon mustard
1 tablespoon kosher salt
2 teaspoons Old Bay seasoning
2 tablespoons lemon juice
1 tablespoon chili paste or sriracha

TO MAKE THE CRAB SALAD:

1. In a large mixing bowl, combine the crab meat, red onion, cucumber, and chives.

2. In a separate bowl, whisk together the mayonnaise, Dijon mustard, kosher salt, Old Bay seasoning, lemon juice, and chili paste or sriracha.

3. Pour the dressing over the crab meat mixture, and stir gently until the ingredients are evenly coated.

4. Chill the crab salad in the refrigerator for at least 30 minutes before serving.

5. When you're ready to serve, remove from the refridgerator.

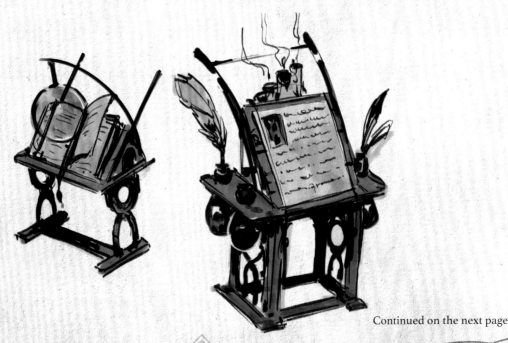

Continued on the next page

BUNS

⅓ cup warm water

½ cup warm milk

1 tablespoon active dry yeast

4 tablespoons sugar

2 tablespoons vegetable or
   canola oil

2½ cups all-purpose flour

½ teaspoon baking powder

¼ teaspoon table salt

3 cups vegetable oil

TO MAKE THE BUNS:

6. Combine warm water, milk, active yeast, sugar, and the 2 tablespoons of oil.

7. Whisk to let the yeast and sugar dissolve; then let sit until the yeast activates or when bubbles form at the top, about 5 to 10 minutes.

8. Combine flour, baking powder, and salt in a stand mixer bowl with a dough hook.

9. Pour the wet ingredients into the dry ingredient mixture. Start on low speed to slowly incorporate all the ingredients together; then increase to medium speed, and mix until it becomes a firm, cohesive dough. Allow the dough to knead for 3 to 4 minutes on medium speed. The dough should be elastic and soft but should not stick to your fingers or the mixing bowl.

10. Take the dough off the hook, and form it into a ball. Place it back in the mixing bowl, cover it with plastic wrap, and let it rise in a warm place until it triples in size, about 2½ hours.

11. Place the risen dough on a clean surface. Sprinkle a small tablespoon of flour on the top, and spread evenly.

12. Roll out the dough until it is ¼ inch thick.

13. Cut the dough into eight to ten 3½-inch circles with a ring mold or with a drinking or wine glass; then remove the excess dough from around the cut circles.

14. Lightly brush or spray oil on one surface of the buns, and fold them in half into a half-moon shape. Gently press each bun with the back of a spoon. Place the buns on a baking tray lined with parchment paper, cover with plastic, and let rest for an additional 30 minutes at room temperature.

15. After the buns have rested, add the remaining three cups of oil to a heavy cast-iron pan or frying pan, heating the oil to 350°F for frying.

16. To cook the buns, gently place a dough circle in the oil and fry until the outside is lightly browned, about 1 to 2 minutes. Flip the bun over, and cook for 1 minute; do not brown the other side. Remove and set on top of paper towels.

17. Place the warm buns on a plate.

18. Fill with the crab salad, and serve.

WESTMARCH NAVY GARLIC PRAWNS

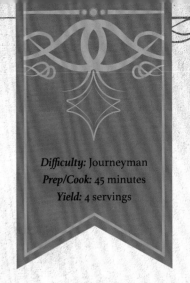

Of course, no small amount of the bustle about the harbor came from the naval ships stationed there. King Cornelius did much to enhance the kingdom's maritime power, fending off the threat of piracy and securing trade at sea. It was a strength that Justinian the Wide-Eyed inherited when he became king after losing his father and brother. As a young man, I recall how far-ranging the selection was at the market, even during Justinian's reign, making for much longer daily errands. I'm sure the perils that befell the city after my time likely changed matters. One matter that has not changed is my appreciation for this efficient, pleasing shrimp dish. Wessel threw in a clever mix of two types of cheeses, well balanced against the butter and the lemon.

Difficulty: Journeyman
Prep/Cook: 45 minutes
Yield: 4 servings

---

1 pound linguine

½ cup extra-virgin olive oil

6 garlic cloves, chopped

1 shallot, finely chopped

1 pound shrimp, peeled, cleaned, and deveined

½ cup white wine

4 tablespoons unsalted butter

Juice of 1 large lemon

1 tablespoon lemon zest

¼ cup fresh parsley, chopped

1 cup grape tomatoes, halved

½ cup Parmesan cheese, grated

½ cup feta cheese, crumbled

1. Cook the linguine in a large pot of salted, boiling water, according to the package instructions, until al dente. Reserve 1 cup of the pasta cooking water.

2. While the pasta is cooking, heat the olive oil in a large skillet over medium heat. Add the chopped garlic and shallot, and cook until fragrant, about 2 to 3 minutes.

3. Add the shrimp to the skillet, and cook until pink and just cooked through, about 3 to 4 minutes.

4. Remove the shrimp from the skillet, and set aside.

5. Add the white wine to the skillet, and bring to a simmer. Cook for about 2 to 3 minutes until the wine has reduced to a third.

6. Stir the butter, lemon juice, lemon zest, and chopped parsley into the sauce.

7. Add the cooked shrimp back into the skillet, along with the halved tomatoes.

8. Add the pasta to the sauce-and-shrimp mixture, and toss in the skillet.

9. Stir in the grated Parmesan cheese and crumbled feta cheese.

10. Serve immediately, topped with additional fresh parsley and lemon zest, if desired.

WESSEL'S VENISON STEW

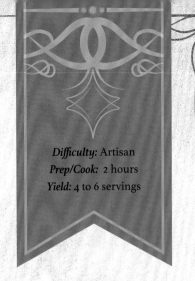

This well-seasoned venison stew originated in Bramwell, but it was so beloved by his lord that Wessel was instructed to learn it, and thus brought it to the tavern. I recall the stew being much loved by patrons of Wolf City as well, but the groundwork of ingredients requires plenty of time for preparation, something Wessel had little to spare. Still, browning the meat beforehand adds a satisfying sizzle of flavor, and the red wine is a savory counterpoint to those browned bits scraped from the bottom of the pot.

Difficulty: Artisan
Prep/Cook: 2 hours
Yield: 4 to 6 servings

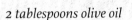

2 tablespoons olive oil

2 pounds venison stew meat, cut into 1-inch cubes

Table salt, to taste

Black pepper, to taste

2 large yellow onions, diced

4 garlic cloves, minced

½ cup red wine

½ cup sundried tomatoes, chopped

2 tablespoons fresh rosemary

6 cups beef broth

4 large carrots, peeled and diced

4 large fingerling potatoes, chopped

1. Heat a large Dutch oven over medium-high heat.

2. Add the olive oil and venison cubes. Season with salt and pepper; then cook until the meat is browned on all sides, about 5 minutes. Remove from the pot, and set aside.

3. In the same pot, add the diced onions and minced garlic. Reduce heat to medium-low. Cook until the onions are translucent, about 5 to 8 minutes.

4. Pour in the red wine, and scrape the bottom of the pot to release any browned bits.

5. Add the sundried tomatoes, rosemary, beef broth, and carrots. Stir to combine.

6. Return the browned venison to the pot, and bring to a boil.

7. Reduce heat to medium-low, and let simmer for 1 hour or until the venison and vegetables are tender. Add in the potatoes, and cook for an additional 30 minutes until the potatoes are cooked through.

8. Serve hot with your favorite crusty bread (page 41).

BLOOD MARSH CHOCOLATE TART

They say only fools dare venture into the Blood Marsh—and they are likely right. When I asked after the origins of this tasty tart, Essen said in a hushed tone that it came from Rakkis's failed search for a mythical city. He described Rakkis's crusaders fending off bogans and bats in order to ascertain the true prize of the ruin at the heart of the Blood Marsh: a smattering of carvings detailing the preparation of this rare treat. As a youth, I thought this quite the rousing tale; as an old man, I can see it was but a fantastic veneer to conceal what was likely a mundane origin. Improbable though his story may be, the tart is worth a (perhaps short) jaunt into that accursed quagmire.

Difficulty: Master
Prep/Cook: 8 hours
Yield: 6 to 8 slices

FILLING

1 cup (2 sticks) plus 1 teaspoon
  salted butter, divided
4 tablespoons water, hot
1 tablespoon instant coffee or
  espresso grounds
¾ cup granulated sugar
14 ounces dark chocolate, chopped
1 tablespoon vanilla
4 egg yolks
5 whole eggs

TOPPING
⅛ cup water
⅛ cup granulated sugar
1 pint fresh raspberries
1 pint fresh blackberries
2 tablespoons cocoa powder

TO MAKE THE FILLING:

1. Preheat the oven to 325°F.

2. Using a teaspoon of butter, grease a 9-inch springform pan. Line the base with parchment paper or a circular silicone mat.

3. Mix the espresso with the hot water until dissolved.

4. Create a double boiler by simmering water in a heavy-bottomed pot, then topping with a metal or glass bowl in which to mix the chocolate.

5. Melt the remaining butter over low heat. Add the sugar and dissolved coffee mix. Stir with a rubber spatula until the sugar has dissolved.

6. Add the chocolate in batches and mix until smooth. Be sure to not overheat the chocolate. Use a thermometer to make sure it doesn't go above 140°F.

7. Remove from heat and place in a stand mixer bowl, or other bowl for use with a hand mixer.

8. Add in the vanilla and egg yolks and quickly whisk into the chocolate mixture. Follow up with the whole eggs. Mix until smooth.

9. Pour the mix into the greased pan and shake to set at the bottom.

10. Bake until the edges are slightly cracked and receding from the edge, about 40 minutes. The center should not be set and should jiggle still.

11. Remove from the oven and place in the refrigerator overnight.

TO MAKE THE TOPPING:

12. In a medium saucepan, bring the water to a boil and add the sugar. Stir to dissolve, and then let it cool.

13. Once cooled, coat the raspberries and blackberries with the simple syrup.

14. Garnish the now-set tart with coated berries, and sift cocoa powder over the top. Slice and serve.

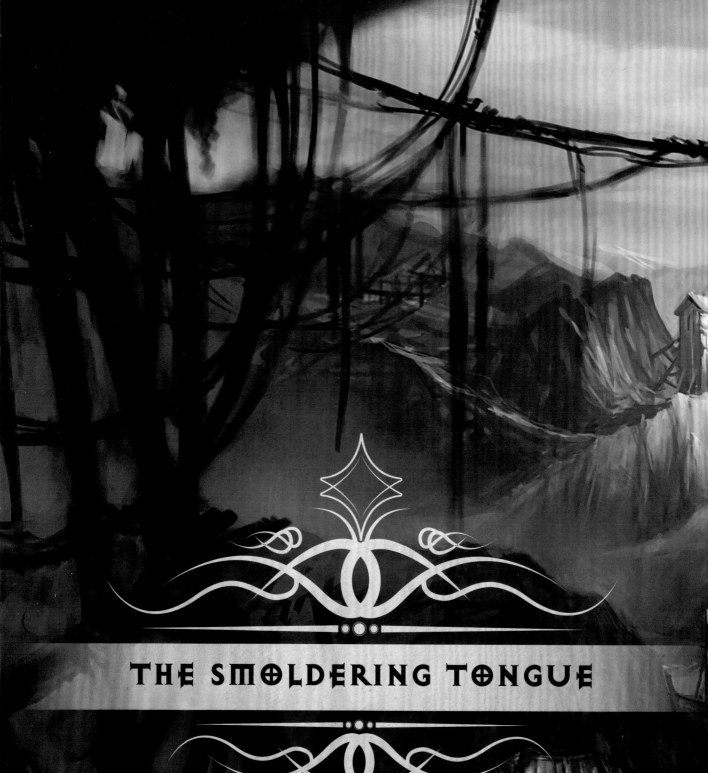

THE SMOLDERING TONGUE

STAALBREAK, THE DREADLANDS

Inveterate travelers do not shy away from exploring ruinous regions, for such places often serve up surprising rewards. I boldly ventured into such a place when I visited the Dreadlands over a half century ago. Once known as the Northern Steppes, these rolling grasslands were blasted to ash when Mount Arreat was torn apart. Yet, in beleaguered Staalbreak—a dreary outpost surrounded by bleak land—I investigated one of the most remarkable eateries.

The Smoldering Tongue it was aptly named, celebrating the visceral thrill of spicy heat as it hit the palate, courtesy of its cook—back then, a woman named Anara. My eyes watered in anticipation as platters of her trademark spiced shredded beef slid down the bar top, infusing the air with cayenne, garlic, and an avocado sauce enlivened with serrano pepper. Most notable were her merguez sausage patties, of which I requested two rounds on first sampling, trying to guess the recipe by mere taste alone. Though much time has passed since I last visited, I have done my best to replicate her recipes here.

ARREAT ROASTED RED PEPPER EGGS

If one is strong-willed enough to reach Staalbreak, then they are adventurous enough to try Anara's peppered eggs. She granted me a taste of the distinctive filling—an amalgam of egg yolk and roasted red pepper, among other things. Dollops were shelled into the halves of a dozen hard-boiled eggs arranged on a tray. When I asked her why she had named them after the mountain, she noted—rather bluntly—that she made them in such quantity that the platters were "piled high as the old mountain"—only to be demolished, much like the mountain was—in the morning rush. I suppose in the face of such devastation, humor is as good a way to cope as any.

Difficulty: Apprentice
Prep/Cook: 1 hour
Yield: 4 servings

---

8 large eggs

¼ cup roasted red peppers

4 tablespoons mayonnaise

1 tablespoon Dijon mustard

2 teaspoons paprika, divided

1 teaspoon table salt

3 chives, chopped small

TO MAKE THE CRUST:

1. Bring a large pot of water to a boil over high heat.

2. Gently lower the eggs into the water, return to a boil, and reduce heat to a low simmer.

3. Cook the eggs for 11 minutes, drain, and place in a large bowl of ice water to sit for 10 minutes.

4. Peel the eggs, and slice in half lengthwise. Gently remove the yolks, and place the yolks in a food processor. Set the whites in the refrigerator to continue chilling.

5. In the food processor, add the roasted red peppers, mayonnaise, mustard, paprika, and salt. Mix until smooth.

6. Transfer the yolk mixture to a pastry bag fitted with a large round tip, or a large plastic bag. If using a resealable bag, squeeze out the air, seal, and snip off a corner.

7. Pipe about 1 tablespoon of filling into the center of each egg white, being careful not to overfill.

8. Garnish with chopped chives on top, and then sprinkle the yolks with paprika.

9. Serve immediately, or cover and refrigerate for up to 1 day.

OWL TRIBE SHREDDED BEEF

Staalbreak was unique for its bridging of two peoples: the barbarians of the Dreadlands, whose ancestral charge was to defend Mount Arreat, and the descendants of Rakkis's northward push spreading the Zakarum faith. Though these groups were not always allied, they came to know peace through various marriages between their peoples over the years. Half of this recipe came to the Smoldering Tongue through the constable's wife, a barbarian of the Owl tribe, with the second half a specialty of the constable himself. It starts with a traditional barbarian dish: flank steak, sliced thin. Before grilling, however, those slices get soaked in the constable's marinade for a full day. The addition of the constable's avocado sauce, with its luscious sting of serrano pepper, made for a rather perfect marriage of flavor. I heard that a horrible plague befell Staalbreak not long after my time there, and that both the constable and his wife were lost in the chaos that followed. I like to think their love lives on in this dish.

Difficulty: Artisan
Prep/Cook: 8 hours
Yield: 4 servings

AVOCADO SAUCE

2 ripe avocados

¼ cup heavy cream

1 bunch cilantro

¼ cup lime juice

½ serrano pepper

1½ teaspoons table salt

BEEF

1 pound flank steak, sliced thin

½ cup soy sauce

¼ cup sriracha sauce

¼ cup chopped scallions, plus
   more for garnishing

3 tablespoons brown sugar

2 tablespoons red chili paste

4 tablespoons minced garlic

2 tablespoons sesame seeds

2 tablespoons sesame oil

1 teaspoon cayenne pepper

1 teaspoon black pepper

TO MAKE THE AVOCADO SAUCE:

1. In a blender or food processor, add the avocados, heavy cream, cilantro, lime juice, serrano, and salt, and blend until creamy. Set aside in the refrigerator.

TO MAKE THE BEEF:

2. Place the flank steak slices in a shallow dish.

3. Mix soy sauce, sriracha sauce, scallions, brown sugar, chili paste, garlic, sesame seeds, sesame oil, cayenne pepper, and pepper together in a bowl.

4. Pour over the steak. Cover with plastic wrap, and refrigerate overnight, for a maximum of 72 hours.

5. Set a grill to 500°F, or place a sauté pan over high heat.

6. Remove the steak slices from the marinade and reserve.

7. Cook the steak on the preheated grill or in the sauté pan until the meat hits an internal temperature of 140°F, about 4 minutes per side on the grill or 6 to 8 minutes in a hot pan.

8. Remove the meat, and set it aside to rest.

9. Pour the remaining marinade into the pan, and reduce until slightly thickened; then pour the marinade over the grilled steak.

10. Garnish with scallions, and serve with the avocado sauce.

GRAY WARDS ONION PIE

I came to know the Gray Wards as perhaps a neighborhood in Staalbreak best avoided. The sick, injured, and wretched of the town were packed in tightly here, each crying out for succor. This recipe comes from the kindly apothecary who serviced the wards. He found that the onion and egg offered strength to those who needed it. For those who choose to attempt this recipe in the kitchen at home, they should keep in mind that other onion varieties can also work, but according to the apothecary from whom this recipe originated, Vidalia onions are best for this particular bake.

Difficulty: Artisan
Prep/Cook: 2 hours
Yield: 6 to 8 slices

PIE CRUST

1¼ cups all-purpose flour

½ tablespoon sugar

¼ teaspoon table salt

8 tablespoons unsalted butter

3 tablespoons ice water

ONION FILLING

3 tablespoons unsalted butter

4 cups thinly sliced Vidalia onion
   or sweet yellow onion
   (about 2 large onions)

1 tablespoon white balsamic
   vinegar

1 teaspoon sugar

3 large eggs, lightly beaten

½ cup heavy cream

1 cup grated Parmesan cheese,
   divided

½ teaspoon table salt

3 sprigs fresh thyme, chopped

TO MAKE THE CRUST:

1. Combine the flour, sugar, and salt in the bowl of a food processor, and pulse 2 to 3 times.

2. Add the butter, and pulse a few times.

3. Add the water, 1 tablespoon at a time, and gently pulse until the dough is formed.

4. Make a flat disk with the dough, cover it with plastic, and refrigerate for 30 minutes to 1 hour.

5. Preheat the oven to 375°F.

6. Roll out the dough on a floured surface until it is ¼ inch thick.

7. Place the dough in a quiche dish, trim the edges, and crimp it with your fingers.

8. Line the shell with parchment paper, and place pie weights on top. If you don't have weights, you can use canned vegetables or uncooked beans.

9. Blind-bake the pie shell for 18 to 20 minutes or until it looks golden brown.

10. Remove the parchment paper and weights, and let the pie shell cool completely.

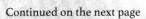

Continued on the next page

TO MAKE THE FILLING:

11. While the crust is baking, melt 3 tablespoons of butter in a large sauté pan, and sauté the onions. When the onions have reached a light brown color, add the balsamic and sugar to finish cooking. Set aside to cool.

12. Whisk together the eggs with the heavy cream until frothy.

13. Add half of the Parmesan cheese, season with salt, and set aside.

14. Evenly distribute the onions on the crust.

15. Pour the egg-and-cream mixture into the crust. Add the chopped thyme, and fold in gently.

16. Bake at 350°F for 20 minutes or until the quiche is golden. Gently shake the pie to ensure that there is no movement, and then allow it to set.

17. Sprinkle the remaining Parmesan cheese on the pie crust.

18. Let the pie cool for at least 10 minutes; then slice and serve.

HARROGATH BLACK GARLIC MUSHROOM ROLL

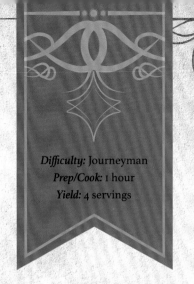

Shadowing Anara in the kitchen, I found that she sought perfection in her food. Anara explained herself while preparing these rolls, which were once made in the barbarian city of Harrogath.

She had seen the aimless look of the barbarians who passed through her door over the years. They had lost much of their culture in the ruin of the mountain, but she knew she could keep one aspect of it alive: through their food. That responsibility drove her to be meticulous—from the mincing and chopping to the skillet work; the caramelization; and the filling of the rolls. I saw even the most surly, hardened member of the Owl tribe crack a smile after taking his first few bites.

Difficulty: Journeyman
Prep/Cook: 1 hour
Yield: 4 servings

4 teaspoons olive oil, divided

1 white onion, diced small

4 cloves black garlic, minced or smashed (alternatively, you can use 4 tablespoons roasted garlic)

5 cups mushrooms, diced small

3 tablespoons soy sauce

8 sprigs fresh thyme, chopped small

¼ cup chopped curly parsley

1 cup cashews

2 to 3 tablespoons nutritional yeast

1 sheet puff pastry

EGG WASH

2 eggs, beaten

2 tablespoons water

1. Heat a large skillet over low heat, and add 2 teaspoons of olive oil.

2. Add the chopped onions and minced garlic to the pan, and cook until soft and lightly browned.

3. Add an additional 2 teaspoons of olive oil. Then add the chopped mushrooms to the pan, and cook until they are caramelized and the liquid has evaporated, about 5 to 7 minutes.

4. Add soy sauce, thyme leaves, and chopped parsley to the pan, and let reduce over medium-low heat until most of the liquid has evaporated, about 4 to 5 minutes. Remove from heat.

5. In a food processor, pulse 1 cup of cashews until they are ground and crumbly.

6. Add the crumbled cashews and 2 to 3 tablespoons of nutritional yeast to the mushroom mixture, and stir to combine.

7. Preheat the oven to 400°F. Roll out a puff pastry sheet on a lightly floured surface, and cut it in half lengthwise.

8. Spoon the mushroom mixture slightly off-center on one half of the puff pastry.

9. Lightly moisten the long edge of the pastry with the egg wash. Lift the long side of the pastry up and over the filling, tucking and rolling it to create a tight roll.

10. Cut the roll into bite-size pieces, about 1 to 1½ inches, and arrange them seam side down on a baking sheet.

11. Brush the rolls with additional egg wash.

12. Place the brushed rolls in the oven and bake until golden brown, about 12 to 15 minutes.

13. Sprinkle with parsley and serve.

RATION'S RESPITE STIR FRY

Anyone who has traveled the Dreadlands knows that the place lives up to its name, for it is truly a land to be dreaded. Something about forced rationing as you make your way through the seemingly endless fields of rubble (flung far and wide from Arreat's destruction) will lead travelers to yearn for even the simplest of dishes. Happily, the Smoldering Tongue offers the best possible version of exactly that. Anara recommends this dish to every traveler who first wanders through her doors; this nutritious, filling, and—most importantly—delicious meal is always a welcome return to civilization.

Difficulty: Journeyman
Prep/Cook: 30 minutes
Yield: 4 servings

4 tablespoons vegetable oil, divided

4 garlic cloves, minced

1 tablespoon ginger, finely grated

1 large red bell pepper, sliced

1 large white onion, sliced

½ cup frozen peas

1 block firm tofu, drained, patted dry, and cut into 1-inch cubes

4 tablespoons cornstarch

2 tablespoons soy sauce

1 tablespoon oyster sauce

1 tablespoon hoisin sauce

2 teaspoons sesame oil

2 cups cooked brown rice

2 tablespoons chopped green onions

2 tablespoons chopped cilantro

1. In a large wok or skillet, heat 1 tablespoon of vegetable oil over medium-high heat.

2. Add the garlic and ginger, and stir-fry for 30 seconds.

3. Add the red bell pepper and onion, and stir-fry for 2 minutes.

4. Add the frozen peas, and continue to stir-fry for another minute.

5. Remove the vegetable mixture from the wok, and set aside.

6. In the same wok, heat 3 tablespoons of vegetable oil.

7. Coat the tofu with the cornstarch, being sure not to break the tofu cubes. Add the tofu cubes to the wok, and stir-fry for 4 to 5 minutes or until browned and crispy on all sides. Drain the remaining oil.

8. Return the vegetable mixture to the wok, and add the soy sauce, oyster sauce, hoisin sauce, and sesame oil.

9. Toss to combine.

10. Cook the brown rice based on package instructions.

11. Serve the stir-fry over a bed of brown rice, topped with chopped green onions and cilantro.

PERFECT PROVISIONS SAUSAGE BITES

I must admit that upon attempting to leave Staalbreak, I only got as far as its forbidding, ice-encrusted bounds on the snow-packed road before quickly realizing I lacked certain provisions needed for comfort in the badlands beyond. My stomach guided me back to the Smoldering Tongue, where I asked Anara for her best recommendation regarding traveling provisions. Minutes later, after feeling sensation return to my thawing fingertips, I found myself loading up on these exquisitely spiced lamb patties.

Difficulty: Artisan
Prep/Cook: 10 hours
Yield: 8 to 10 sausage patties

¼ teaspoon ground fennel seeds

1 teaspoon ground cumin

½ teaspoon ground cinnamon

½ teaspoon ground coriander

¼ teaspoon ground turmeric

3 garlic cloves, minced

2 tablespoons harissa

1 tablespoon tomato paste

1 pound ground lamb
 (or lean ground beef)

1 tablespoon baking soda

1 teaspoon table salt

2 tablespoons olive oil

1. Using a food processor or mortar and pestle, mix the fennel, cumin, cinnamon, coriander, turmeric, garlic, harissa, and tomato paste.

2. In a medium bowl, combine the spice mix with the ground lamb, and mix thoroughly. The mix should be a deep red. Then sprinkle in the baking soda and salt, and mix again.

3. Cover, and place in the refrigerator for at least 8 hours (up to 72 hours).

4. Remove, and form 8 to 10 sausage patties that are about 2 ounces each, or about the size of a lemon.

5. Heat a skillet to medium-high heat, and add the olive oil.

6. Cook the patties until the internal temperature is 160°F, about 6 to 8 minutes per side.

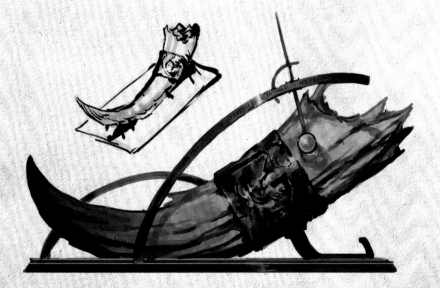

BLASPHEMOUS APRICOT CAKE

Many denizens of Staalbreak still follow Akarat, whose teachings would give rise to the Zakarum church. Anara shared that perhaps the highest praise she ever received came from a local patron who noted—in barely a whisper—that he would renounce Akarat in an unholy instant if it meant unfettered access to her apricot cake. Hence, the cake was aptly named. After trying it myself, I understand why it became a sweet staple of the public house.

Difficulty: Artisan
Prep/Cook: 50 minutes
Yield: 6 to 8 servings

APRICOT GLAZE

⅓ cup apple juice

3 tablespoons sugar

6 ounces apricots, diced small

CAKE

½ cup plus 3 tablespoons unsalted butter, room temperature, divided

¼ cup raw sugar

½ cup granulated sugar

2 eggs, with whites and yolks separated

¼ teaspoon cream of tartar

1 teaspoon almond extract

1 teaspoon lemon zest

¼ teaspoon table salt

1½ cups flour

2 teaspoons baking powder

1 cup buttermilk

One 12-ounce package dried apricot halves

¼ cup sliced almonds

TO MAKE THE GLAZE:

1. Combine the juice and sugar in a small pot. Bring to a boil over medium heat; then reduce the temperature to a low simmer.

2. Add the apricots to the pot, and simmer until the mix makes a syrup; set aside.

TO MAKE THE CAKE:

3. Grease a springform pan with 3 tablespoons room temperature butter and raw sugar.

4. Preheat oven to 375°F.

5. Whisk the egg whites with the cream of tartar until stiff peaks form.

6. Using a mixer, cream together the remaining butter, granulated sugar, almond extract, lemon zest, and salt.

7. Add the yolks of the eggs one at a time, and continue to mix until blended.

8. Slowly add the flour and baking powder using a sifter.

9. Add the buttermilk, and mix until the batter is combined.

10. Then fold in the egg whites.

11. Layer the bottom of the pan with apricot halves, cut side down. Press them in very slightly.

12. Pour the mixture into the pan; spread it evenly, and fill two-thirds of the way—do not fill completely.

13. Bake until a toothpick inserted into the center of the cakes comes out slightly clean (totally clean means the cakes are overbaked), about 22 to 25 minutes.

14. Carefully remove the cake from the pan, and allow to cool for at least 20 minutes.

15. Serve by pouring a tablespoon of glaze over the cake and garnish with the sliced almonds.

THE HANGED MAN

MENESTAD, FRACTURED PEAKS

Can you imagine walking into a tavern called the Hanged Man? Welcome to the frigid Fractured Peaks, a land with its own ominous name. This snowy, rocky region, barely habitable, is home to packs of hungry wolves, vicious khazra, and a steady flow of pilgrims in search of sacred truths. Frankly, I can think of no truth more sacred than the epiphany provided by a skillet of pork cutlets in a sherry cream sauce. That sort of enlightenment can be found in the rugged village of Menestad, where traveling devotees take a final rest before pushing on to Kyovashad and the Cathedral of Light itself.

Menestad is home to the Hanged Man—a different kind of holy sanctum; a place to nourish one's soul, especially after days navigating precarious crags and desolate ruins. Knights and pilgrims gather here to drink and gamble, and to bluster over sumptuous repast. Tribulations fade as cupbearers serve up ale and the inn's popular starter delicacy, a tasty sausage and apple hand pie. Follow that up with the aforementioned pork cutlets or a rabbit fricassee, add baby carrots and parsnips . . . and soon, any lingering road woes are scattered like boot pebbles—at least until it's time to brave the wintry wilds once more. On the following pages are my Hanged Man's recipe recommendations.

OSSO'S JERKY AND SPROUTS

Jerky is very popular in these parts. It is a survival food for rugged highland travel, to be sure. However, jerky doesn't have to be tough and tasteless. The kitchen of the Hanged Man is run by a no-nonsense fellow named Osso, the lone survivor of a traveling caravan brutally set upon by wargs. Prior to that, he spent years on the road as a cook for his comrades, and early on discovered how to turn jerky into something palatable. Osso's solution: fry it with Brussels sprouts and slather with a hot chili sauce, honey, butter, and salt. These savory vittles are ideal to take on a trek through the mountains.

Difficulty: Journeyman
Prep/Cook: 30 minutes
Yield: 4 servings

---

3 tablespoons vegetable oil
20 Brussels sprouts,
  halved lengthwise
2½ ounces beef jerky,
  sliced to about ⅛ inch
3 tablespoons sriracha
2 tablespoons honey
2 tablespoons unsalted butter
½ tablespoon table salt

1. Set a large frying pan to medium-low heat, and line the pan with oil.

2. Carefully place as many Brussels sprouts as possible in the pan, keeping them flat side down.

3. Allow the Brussels sprouts to slowly, heavily darken on one side; this should take about 10 minutes per batch.

4. When the sprouts have become tender, remove them from the heat and place them in a large bowl.

5. Reduce the heat in the pan to low, and add the jerky. Cook until slightly tender, about 2 minutes. Remove from heat and add the jerky to the bowl with the Brussels sprouts. Add sriracha, honey, butter, and salt.

6. Toss until the Brussels sprouts are evenly coated, and serve.

ISKREN'S JERKY DIP

The proprietor at the Hanged Man—Iskren, last I knew—was an enterprising fellow. He saw opportunity in Osso's jerky and suggested an evolution of the dish, something that would keep patrons seated at the bar, ordering ale. Osso started with his standard beef jerky and added minced garlic, red pepper flakes, and smoked paprika to a creamy blend. The result: a zesty dip that revitalizes any exhausted soul. I have seen unsuspecting guests widen their eyes in astonishment with the first bite, and, as Iskren desired, order a brisk stout to counter the kick.

Difficulty: Apprentice
Prep/Cook: 30 minutes
Yield: 15 ounces of dip

---

8 ounces soft cream cheese
6 ounces whole-fat Greek yogurt
1 tablespoon olive oil
6½ ounces spicy beef jerky
2 garlic cloves, minced
1 shallot, minced
½ cup chopped walnuts, about
⅛-inch pieces
1 tablespoon chopped thyme
1 tablespoon red pepper flakes
½ tablespoon freshly
cracked black pepper
2 teaspoons smoked paprika
2 sprigs thyme for garnishing

1. In a large bowl, place cream cheese and yogurt. Using a hand mixer or whisk, whip until creamy; set aside.

2. Place a medium sauté pan over medium heat.

3. Add the oil to the pan, followed by the jerky, garlic, shallot, and walnuts.

4. Cook, moving the mix constantly, until garlic and shallots are fragrant, about 2 minutes; then remove from heat.

5. While the pan is still warm, add the chopped thyme and red pepper flakes; mix, and then add to the cream cheese mixture.

6. Mix until everything is well incorporated, and scrape into a serving bowl.

7. To garnish, add freshly cracked pepper, sprinkle the paprika, and crisscross the thyme sprigs over the top.

MONK'S SAUSAGE AND APPLE TITHE

As I sat playing cards with a motley assortment of uncouth locals one night, an ashen-faced monk approached Iskren at the bar. I did not know it at the time, but this visit was a shakedown of sorts—traveling monks serve as tithe collectors for the Cathedral of Light back in Kyovashad. I was surprised to see Osso himself emerge from the kitchen. He set a plate with two perfect hand pies before the priest, who then consumed them hungrily. After chasing the pies with a splash of ale, the holy man waved his hand in a sort of benediction—*may you walk in the path of the Light*—and left.

Difficulty: Artisan
Prep/Cook: 1 hour, 15 minutes
Yield: 6 pies

---

1 pound sweet Italian sausage, casings removed

¼ cup diced onion

1 medium Granny Smith apple, peeled and diced

1 garlic clove, minced

1 teaspoon dried thyme

1 teaspoon table salt

1 teaspoon black pepper

2 tablespoons sherry cream

One 14-ounce package frozen puff pastry

EGG WASH

1 egg, beaten

1 tablespoon water

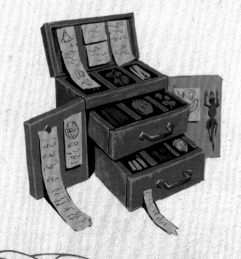

1. Preheat oven to 400°F. Line a baking sheet with parchment paper.

2. In a large skillet over medium heat, cook the sausage, breaking it up with a spatula, until browned and cooked through, about 8 to 10 minutes. Drain any excess grease.

3. Add the onion, apple, garlic, thyme, salt, and pepper to the skillet with the sausage. Cook until the onion is soft and translucent, about 5 minutes.

4. Add the sherry, and cook for 2 minutes. Set aside to cool.

5. On a lightly floured surface, roll out one of the puff pastry to a thickness of ⅛ inch. Cut the dough into 4-inch circles. Repeat with the other dough disk.

6. Spoon 2 tablespoons of the sausage mixture onto one half of each circle, leaving a ½-inch border around the edge.

7. Combine the beaten egg and water. Brush the edges of the dough with the egg wash, and fold the other half of the dough over the filling, pressing the edges together to seal. Use a fork to crimp the edges. You can also pinch or use a fold-and-flip technique.

8. Brush the top of each hand pie with the remaining egg wash. Cut two slits in the top of each hand pie to allow steam to escape.

9. Bake the hand pies for 15 to 20 minutes or until golden brown. Alternatively, you can air-fry at 350°F for 4 minutes per side.

PILGRIM'S MUSHROOM AND CARROT POTTAGE

Osso would often loudly lament of traveling pilgrims downing his carefully crafted meals with barely a moment to savor them. Having navigated the winding mountain passes and narrowly avoided a frigid end myself, I can understand the welcome embrace a warm meal can be amid a long journey. The poor fellows claimed it was their proximity to the Cathedral of Light returning life to their limbs, but . . . as a non-believer I would say Osso's pottage is more likely the miracle they are experiencing. Those poor souls were simply unaccustomed to seasoning.

Difficulty: Journeyman
Prep/Cook: 1 hour
Yield: 6 servings

2 pounds mushrooms, thinly sliced

6 medium carrots, peeled and
    sliced into rounds

2 Yukon Gold potatoes, diced to
    ½ inch

1 large onion, diced to ½ inch

4 garlic cloves, minced

4 tablespoons olive oil

2 tablespoons flour

2 teaspoons dried thyme

1 teaspoon dried rosemary

1 tablespoon table salt

½ teaspoon black pepper

2 cups vegetable broth

½ cup heavy cream (use almond or
    coconut cream as a replacement)

1. Preheat oven to 400°F.

2. In a large bowl, combine mushrooms, carrots, potatoes, onion, garlic, and olive oil. Toss until the vegetables are coated in oil. Season with salt and pepper.

3. Spread the mixture in a single layer on a baking sheet, and bake for 25 to 30 minutes or until the vegetables are tender and slightly browned. Reserve the oil and drippings from the pan.

4. In a large pot, heat the flour over medium heat, and stir constantly until it becomes a light brown color. Be sure to lower the heat if you notice any burning spots.

5. Add the roasted vegetables and drippings into the flour mix, and stir together until the vegetables are coated and all the flour has vanished, creating a roux.

6. Add the thyme, rosemary, salt, pepper, and vegetable broth. Bring to a boil, and then stir, being sure to scrape the bottom until the mix begins to thicken.

7. Reduce heat, and bring it to a low simmer for 15 to 20 minutes. Check for seasoning.

8. Once thickened, stir in the heavy cream, and continue cooking for an additional 10 minutes until heated. Serve.

KNIGHTS PENITENT PORK CUTLETS

Ah, I must confess that I particularly enjoy this recipe, though Osso only served it from time to time, and only to his favorite patrons due to its fine ingredients. Its name comes from the Knights Penitent, who serve the interests of the Cathedral of Light. Though these knights operate through seeking penance for their sins, Osso found their grim methods off-putting, and bent his skills toward making a dish so sinfully delicious that the knights could not partake in it. The result was these tender pork cutlets. I must admit, if enjoying rich food makes me a sinner, I am not sure I wish to be absolved.

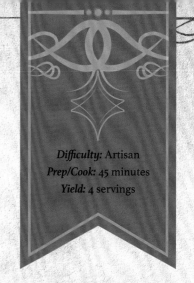

Difficulty: Artisan
Prep/Cook: 45 minutes
Yield: 4 servings

Four 6-ounce boneless pork cutlets
Table salt, to taste
Black pepper, to taste
½ cup all-purpose flour
2 tablespoons olive oil
1 shallot, minced
3 garlic cloves, minced
½ cup dry sherry
1½ cups chicken broth
½ cup heavy cream
2 tablespoons unsalted butter

1. Season the pork cutlets with salt and pepper on both sides. Dredge each cutlet in flour, shaking off any excess.

2. In a large skillet over medium heat, heat the olive oil. Add the pork cutlets, and cook until golden brown on both sides, about 2 to 3 minutes per side.

3. Remove the pork from the skillet, and set aside.

4. In the same skillet, add the minced shallot and garlic. Cook until fragrant, about 1 minute.

5. Add the sherry to the skillet; cook, stirring constantly, until reduced by half, about 3 minutes.

6. Add the chicken broth and heavy cream to the skillet, stirring to combine. Bring the mixture to a simmer for about 2 minutes.

7. Return the pork cutlets to the skillet, and spoon the sauce over them. Cook until the sauce has thickened slightly, about 5 minutes.

8. Remove the pork cutlets from the skillet, and keep warm. In the same skillet, whisk in the unsalted butter until melted and well combined.

9. Serve the pork cutlets with the sherry cream sauce.

WARG'S STICKY BAKED CHICKEN OFFERING

Entering the Hanged Man one night, we heard the howls of a pack of wargs not too far outside the city gate. "Worry not," Osso assured me, "for I have a secret weapon." Methodically collecting ingredients from the kitchen, I watched in awe as he prepared a heaping platter of sticky, smoked chicken wings. This was, he explained, a dish that he had prepared the night his caravan had been attacked by the beasts. They had been so distracted by the delicious smell that they had ignored the cook altogether.

Difficulty: Artisan
Prep/Cook: 3 hours
Yield: 12 wings

3 pounds chicken wings

MARINADE
½ teaspoon toasted sesame oil
2 tablespoons lemon juice
2 tablespoons Chinese cooking wine (can substitute mirin or dry sherry)
2 tablespoons light or all-purpose soy sauce
3 tablespoons brown sugar or honey
2 tablespoons hoisin sauce
1 tablespoon oyster sauce
1 tablespoon chili garlic sauce or sambal oelek (adjust to desired spiciness)
4 garlic cloves, minced
1 tablespoon ginger, finely grated
½ teaspoon Chinese five-spice powder

GLAZING SAUCE
2 teaspoons cornstarch
2 teaspoons water
Reserved marinade
¼ cup cilantro, chopped

1. Combine all the ingredients for the marinade in a bowl, and mix well. Reserve ¼ cup of the marinade.

2. Place the chicken wings in a large bowl, and pour the marinade over them.

3. Toss to ensure that the wings are well coated.

4. Cover the wings, and refrigerate for at least 2 hours, or overnight for best results.

5. Preheat oven or grill to 400°F.

6. Bake the wings on a roasting sheet until cooked through and crispy, and they have reached an internal temperature of 165°F, about 20 to 25 minutes. Alternatively, you can grill the wings for 8 to 10 minutes.

7. While the wings cook, place the reserved marinade in a small pot, and bring to a simmer.

8. In a small cup, mix the cornstarch and water to make a slurry. Add the mixture to the simmering marinade, and stir until thickened. Toss in the cilantro, and mix.

9. Place the wings on a large, flat plate. Drizzle sauce over the top, and serve.

SNOWMELT RICOTTA PANCAKES

I once asked Osso why he chose to stay in these rugged, cold, unforgiving mountains, so far from the clear sky and open sea. With the Cathedral of Light based in Kyovashad, he said he has never had steadier business—both literally and figuratively. (He noted it was nice to work in a kitchen that did not violently rock side to side on the road.) He also preferred the effects of the high altitude on his baking. "Up here," he told me, "it is easier to make my favorite dessert—ricotta pancakes. Besides, I can always find wild berries for the compote."

Difficulty: Artisan
Prep/Cook: 40 minutes
Yield: 12 pancakes

PANCAKES

1½ cups all-purpose flour
3 tablespoons sugar
2 teaspoons baking powder
¼ teaspoon baking soda
¼ teaspoon table salt
1 cup ricotta cheese
¾ cup milk
2 large eggs
2 tablespoons unsalted butter, melted
1 teaspoon vanilla extract
Zest of 1 medium lemon

COMPOTE

2 cups fresh blueberries
¼ cup freshly squeezed lemon juice
¼ cup sugar
Pinch table salt
1 tablespoon cornstarch
1 tablespoon water

TO MAKE THE PANCAKES:

1. In a large bowl, whisk together the flour, sugar, baking powder, baking soda, and salt.

2. In a separate bowl, whisk together the ricotta cheese, milk, eggs, melted butter, vanilla extract, and lemon zest until smooth.

3. Pour the wet mixture into the dry mixture, and stir until combined.

4. Heat a large nonstick skillet over medium heat and grease with nonstick spray or butter.

5. Using a measuring cup, pour batter into the skillet, spreading it out slightly to form a 4-inch round pancake.

6. Cook until the surface is bubbly and the edges start to look dry, about 2 to 3 minutes.

7. Flip the pancake and cook until the bottom is golden brown, about 1 to 2 minutes more.

8. Repeat with remaining batter. Once complete, serve with the compote.

TO MAKE THE COMPOTE:

9. In a medium saucepan, combine the blueberries, lemon juice, sugar, and salt.

10. Cook over medium heat until the blueberries start to burst and release their juices, about 5 minutes.

11. In a small bowl, whisk together the cornstarch and water until smooth.

12. Stir the cornstarch mixture into the blueberry mixture, and cook until the sauce thickens, about 2 to 3 minutes.

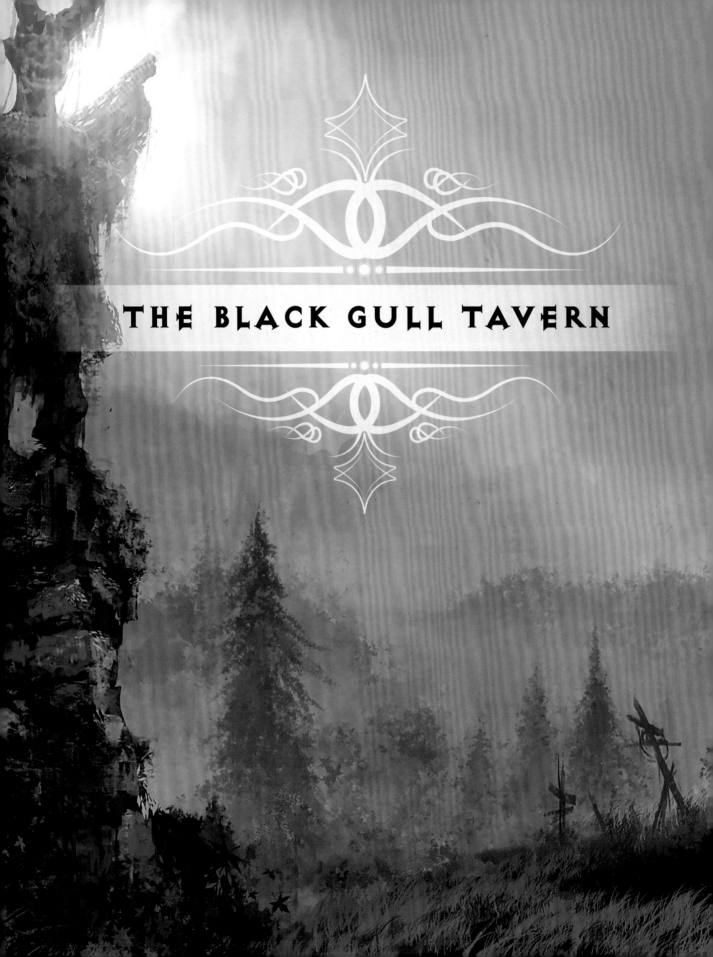

THE BLACK GULL TAVERN

MAROWEN, SCOSGLEN

I once heard a fellow wanderer refer to coastal Scosglen as a feral nightmare. She was not wrong, of course—breakers from the pitiless Frozen Sea pound those northern beaches with seaweed, kelp, and an unsettling number of rotting carcasses. That is hardly the worst of it, though. The ancestral home of the druids also suffers from a chilling scourge of drownings and disappearances—villagers said to go missing, preceded only by the tolling of bells . . .

However, this land is verdant and beautiful, so tied as it is to nature and the sea. Overlooking this untamed shoreline is the fisherman's port of Marowen, gateway to the sea from Scosglen's rugged hinterland. Travelers join the local fishing crews in the warm firelight of Marowen's Black Gull Tavern. This earthy inn features a surprisingly sophisticated menu of ocean-inspired specialties—including steamed mussels, a succulent smoked haddock and rice dish, and golden-brown salmon cakes. Finish any of these meals off with a bowl of poached pears and a good night's sleep, and one might feel ready for anything, even Scosglen's harsh, unforgiving elements. Fortunately, you can enjoy the following recipes without the peril it takes to reach the doorstep of the Black Gull.

WEREBEAR SALMON CAKES AND TÚL DÚLRA BREAD

Difficulty: Apprentice
Prep/Cook: 30 minutes
Yield: 4 cakes

As a well-traveled old man, I am not one to be easily taken in by a tale. That said, I heard the same story from many a wide-eyed patron, newly arrived from the inner woodlands. Folk talk of certain people—druids by the way some tell it—who become terrible beasts when giving in to their primal rage. I have heard much of werewolves (and have also never given much credence to them,) but people transfiguring into *bears*? This was entirely unfamiliar to me. Whether it be wolves, bears, or just plain druids roaming Scosglen, I suspect they all would dine on these fine, flaky salmon cakes. And if that weren't enough, few things are more satisfying on a damp day in Marowen than a good bite of the Black Gull's warm, perfectly toasted garlic bread.

SALMON CAKES

1 pound salmon, skin removed,
   cooked, and flaked

¼ cup shallots, finely chopped

2 tablespoons chives,
   finely chopped

2 tablespoons sour cream

1 egg, lightly beaten

¼ cup breadcrumbs

Table salt, to taste

Black pepper, to taste

1 tablespoon olive oil

TÚR DÚLRA BREAD

1 baguette, sliced ¼ inch thick

4 tablespoons unsalted butter,
   melted

2 tablespoons olive oil

2 tablespoons freshly squeezed
   lemon juice

2 tablespoons sugar

1 teaspoon lemon zest

¼ teaspoon black pepper

¼ teaspoon cayenne pepper

TO MAKE THE SALMON CAKES:

1. In a mixing bowl, combine salmon, shallots, chives, sour cream, egg, breadcrumbs, salt, and pepper. Mix until well combined. Add more breadcrumbs if the mix is too wet.

2. Form the mixture into 8 equal patties.

3. Heat the olive oil in a nonstick pan over medium heat.

4. Cook the patties for 2 to 3 minutes on each side or until golden brown.

5. Place on a plate lined with paper towels and serve.

You can also use packaged or canned salmon.

TO MAKE THE TÚR DÚLRA BREAD

6. Preheat oven to 400°F.

7. Arrange baguette slices on a baking sheet.

8. Brush both sides of the slices with melted butter.

9. Bake until crisp and golden brown, about 10 to 12 minutes.

10. In a small bowl, whisk together olive oil, lemon juice, sugar, lemon zest, pepper, and cayenne pepper.

11. While the toast is still warm, brush the mixture over both sides of the slices.

12. Sprinkle with salt to taste, and serve immediately.

FROZEN SEA STEAMED MUSSELS

While some in Scosglen place great faith in the druids and their ability to protect the land, there are those who whisper of a terrible evil prowling the coast. Its presence is preceded by the tolling of bells and the smell of brine, and it can vanish entire settlements in a single moonless night. Where these people go, none can say for certain. The mystery frightened me such that my stay at the Black Gull was not lengthy, though the rare troves of shellfish around Marowen kept me just a bit longer.

When working with mussels, make sure you start with those that are closed tight and have that fresh, briny sea smell. If any mussel shells are open before cooking, simply give them a tap—if they close within half a minute, they're still alive and usable. However, if they do not close, discard them, and swiftly dispose of any whose shells did not open during cooking. These were likely dead from the start and thus unfit to eat.

Difficulty: Journeyman
Prep/Cook: 25 minutes
Yield: 6 servings

4 slices bacon, chopped

1 large shallot (about ½ cup), finely chopped

4 garlic cloves, minced

½ cup sherry cream

1 cup heavy cream

2 tablespoons chopped fresh parsley

2 tablespoons chopped fresh thyme

1 tablespoon table salt

1 teaspoon black pepper

2 pounds fresh mussels, scrubbed and debearded

1. In a large pot, cook the bacon over medium heat until crispy.

2. Remove with a slotted spoon, and set aside.

3. Add shallots and garlic to the pot, and cook until softened, about 3 minutes.

4. Pour in the sherry, and simmer until reduced by half, about 5 minutes.

5. Stir in the heavy cream, parsley, thyme, salt, and pepper. Bring to a simmer.

6. Add the mussels to the pot, cover, and steam until mussels have opened, about 5 to 7 minutes.

7. Discard any mussels that do not open; they are not safe to eat.

8. Reduce the sherry cream sauce until slightly thickened.

9. Place the mussels in bowls, top with the sherry cream sauce, sprinkle with the crispy bacon, and serve.

TAVISH'S KEDGEREE

This recipe is a testament to the value of tradition. People of Scosglen have been eating kedgeree for centuries, perhaps longer. The fishers of Marowen know it well, as many prepare it in their own homes. Tavish, the cook, has a version that maintains the fundamentals yet still turns the conventional fish, rice, and chopped egg dish into its own distinctive delicacy. First, the kitchen poaches haddock that has been smoked in order to achieve an earthy, fuller flavor in the fish. Next, sautéed onion, garlic, and curry bring a mild tang to the rice base. Finally, the garam masala—a delicious blend of spices—adds a terrific sensation to the entire endeavor.

Difficulty: Journeyman
Prep/Cook: 45 minutes
Yield: 6 to 8 servings

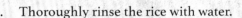

1 cup basmati rice

¼ cup table salt

1 pound smoked haddock, filleted

2 eggs

2 tablespoons olive oil

1 small onion, finely chopped

1 tablespoon garlic, finely chopped

1 teaspoon curry powder

1 teaspoon garam masala

2 tablespoons unsalted butter

2 tablespoons parsley, chopped

1. Thoroughly rinse the rice with water.

2. Cook the rice according to the time on the package instructions.

3. Add 2 quarts of water and the salt to a large pan, set to medium heat (160°F), and poach the smoked haddock fillets for 10 minutes.

4. Remove the fish with a slotted spoon, and peel off the skin.

5. Bring the water back to a simmer and boil the eggs until hard-boiled (about 8 minutes).

6. Remove the eggs, peel, and cut into quarters.

7. Place a large sauté pan over medium heat, and add the oil.

8. Cook onion and garlic in oil until soft, about 1 minute.

9. Add in curry powder and garam masala, and stir-fry for a minute to toast the spices.

10. Add the cooked rice, and cook until heated through.

11. Add the flaked haddock and the butter. Fold in until mixed well.

12. Top the pan with the quartered eggs.

13. Serve hot, garnished with chopped parsley.

FOREFATHER'S VENISON MEATBALLS

During my time at the Black Gull, I was surprised to learn about the ancestral ties between druid and barbarian. Apparently, the barbarians and druids were once part of a single people, united under Bul-Kathos, the barbarian king. Bul-Kathos thought to defend the land and its people through martial prowess, but as time passed, a sect led by the druid forebear, Fiacla-Géar (I have also heard him called Vasily by some townsfolk), sought another way. He brought his followers to Scosglen to hone their connection with the natural world, and through finding such harmony, defend it. This dish honors those shared roots, particularly the hunting of wild game.

Difficulty: Journeyman
Prep/Cook: 1 hour
Yield: 18 to 24 meatballs

SWEET TOMATO SAUCE

¼ cup whole currants

½ cup warm water

One 14.5-ounce can crushed tomatoes

½ cup toasted pine nuts

1 teaspoon table salt

¼ cup honey

¼ cup parsley, roughly chopped

MEATBALLS

½ cup panko breadcrumbs

2 pounds ground venison

¼ cup ground feta

3 tablespoons ras el hanout seasoning

⅓ cup Parmesan cheese

2 tablespoons table salt

2 large eggs

3 garlic cloves, minced

2 medium red onions, diced small

1 tablespoon vegetable oil

2 tablespoons olive oil

TO MAKE THE SWEET TOMATO SAUCE:

1. In a small bowl, soak the currants in the warm water to soften, about 10 minutes.

2. In a medium saucepan, heat the crushed tomatoes over medium heat. Stir until the water is dissolved and bubbling, about 6 minutes.

3. Add currants, toasted pine nuts, salt, and honey, and mix.

4. Bring the tomato mixture to a simmer and cook, stirring occasionally until the sauce has thickened, about 10 to 15 minutes.

5. Remove from heat and stir in the parsley.

TO MAKE THE MEATBALLS:

6. In a large mixing bowl, combine the breadcrumbs, ground venison, feta, ras el hanout, Parmesan cheese, salt, eggs, garlic, and red onions until well mixed.

7. Preheat the oven to 350°F. Wet your hands with cold water to prevent sticking. Grab small amounts of the mixture and roll them into ½-inch balls. You can also use a 2-ounce ice cream scoop.

8. Heat a large skillet over medium-high heat and add 1 tablespoon of vegetable oil. Once the oil is hot, add the meatballs and cook until they are browned on all sides, working in batches to not overcrowd the pan.

9. Grease a medium baking sheet with olive oil. Place the browned meatballs on the sheet.

10. Bake the meatballs until they are fully cooked through, with an internal temperature of 160°F, about 20 to 22 minutes.

11. Remove the meatballs from the oven and place in a serving dish. Coat them with the sauce and serve.

TÚR DÚLRA SALT AND PEPPER CHICKEN AND FIREBREAK BRAISED GREENS

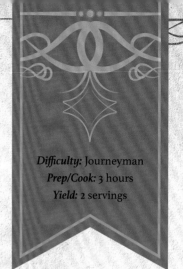

Difficulty: Journeyman
Prep/Cook: 3 hours
Yield: 2 servings

Though the druids seem to prefer the wilds and their colleges (where they hone their magic and connection to nature), it is not uncommon to see them come up the coast to Marowen. In order to make some extra coin during my own visit, I lent my skill to Tavish. These old hands are not as steady as they once were, and serving the meal to a hulking druid, I nearly dropped the plate into his lap. He said not a word, but instead took my hands. To my amazement, the swelling and pain in my knuckles diminished, and the slight shake in my hand vanished for the better part of a fortnight. I have no idea what he did, but Tavish said druidic magic was most likely at work.

BRAISED GREENS

4 pounds collard greens

1 large onion, diced

6 cups chicken broth

1½ tablespoons table salt

1½ tablespoons lemon pepper

3 tablespoons minced garlic

3 tablespoons apple cider vinegar

CHICKEN

1 cup all-purpose flour

2 teaspoons table salt

2 teaspoons black pepper

1 teaspoon Chinese five-spice

*1½ pounds boneless, skinless
   chicken thighs or breasts*

2 tablespoons vegetable oil

4 garlic cloves, minced

2 teaspoons ginger, grated.

½ teaspoon red pepper flakes

2 green onions, sliced

1 medium lemon, cut into wedges.

TO MAKE THE GREENS:

1. Remove the stems from the greens. Add all ingredients to a slow cooker and set to high. The greens will reach the top, but they will slowly break down.

2. Cook on high for 1 hour, then move to low setting for 2½ hours, taking care to stir once per hour.

3. Add additional seasoning if desired and serve.

TO MAKE THE CHICKEN:

4. In a large bowl, whisk together the flour, salt, pepper, and Chinese five-spice powder.

5. Add the chicken, cut into 1-inch pieces, and toss until well coated.

6. In a large skillet, heat the vegetable oil over medium-high heat.

7. Add the chicken pieces and cook for 10 to 12 minutes or until browned and crispy.

8. Add the garlic, ginger, and red pepper flakes to the skillet, and cook for 30 seconds or until fragrant.

9. Stir in the green onions and cook for 1 to 2 minutes or until softened.

10. Allow the chicken to rest for 4 minutes and serve with lemon wedges on the side.

HIGHLANDS RABBIT FRICASSEE

One need only traverse this wild land to know its horrors: the splintered remains of a carriage found on the roadside; a bloodied camp torn to shreds by a grisly predator; an ancient ruin beset by mournful wailing. Perhaps the most frightful occurrences come from the small farms. Protection is scarce outside the city walls, and it is not uncommon to find fields and homesteads torn asunder overnight, victim to one sorrowful attack or another. It is a reminder that the Scosglen wilds are a hard land in which humanity is often the prey of some greater hunter. However, while we yet live and eat and hunt, this fricassee is a lavish improvement upon the standard rabbit stew . . . one worth savoring for as long as possible.

Difficulty: Master
Prep/Cook: 1.5 hours
Yield: 4 servings

---

2 pounds rabbit meat, cut into front and hind, leg, and saddle with the ribcage removed.

Table salt, to taste

Black pepper, to taste

½ cup all-purpose flour

2 large eggs, beaten

¼ cup olive oil

½ cup shallots, minced

4 garlic cloves, minced

1 pound parsnips, peeled and chopped into 1-inch pieces

1 cup dry white wine

1 cup chicken or rabbit broth

1 bouquet garni (fresh thyme, bay leaf, and parsley tied together with string)

1 cup heavy cream

1 pound baby carrots, washed and trimmed

2 tablespoons unsalted butter

1. Season the rabbit pieces with salt and pepper.

2. Place half of the flour in a shallow dish, place the beaten eggs in another shallow dish, and place the remaining flour into a third shallow dish.

3. Coat each piece of rabbit in flour, shaking off the excess. Dip each piece in the beaten eggs and then back in the flour.

4. Heat the olive oil in a large, heavy-bottomed skillet over medium-high heat. Add the rabbit pieces, and cook until golden brown, about 4 minutes on each side. Remove the rabbit from the skillet and set aside.

5. Add the shallots, garlic, and parsnips to the same skillet, and cook until fragrant, about 2 minutes.

6. Add the wine and broth to the skillet, and bring to a boil.

7. Add the bouquet garni; then reduce the heat to medium-low, and let the mixture simmer for 15 minutes.

8. Stir in the heavy cream and return the rabbit to the skillet, set the heat to low simmer.

9. Add the baby carrots and continue to cook until the carrots are tender and the sauce has thickened, about 25 – 30 minutes. Be sure to stir the bottom

10. Remove the bouquet garni from the skillet and stir in the butter.

11. Cook until the rabbit has reached an internal temperature of 160°F; then serve.

HINTERLAND POACHED PEARS

Difficulty: Artisan
Prep/Cook: 40 minutes
Yield: 4 servings

I will not say I much lamented over leaving Marowen—in fact, all of Scosglen—far behind me. The relative isolation of the coastal towns (besides the way residents of these settlements so abruptly disappear) and the many threats of khazra and fallen felt too treacherous for my tastes. Even the simple, though numerous, quillrats filled me with a deep sense of unease. Perhaps the only thing more terrifying than staying, though, was the thought of leaving. I recall Tavish slid a bowl of these pears to me, as a scream cracked the night, and said, "Enjoy delicious things while you can, my friend."

3 cups water

2 cups sugar

1 vanilla bean, split lengthwise, or
   1 tablespoon vanilla extract

3 cinnamon sticks

2 anise stars

4 ripe but firm pears, peeled,
   halved, and cored

Juice from 1 medium lemon

1 medium lemon, thinly sliced

Fresh mint leaves for garnishing

1. In a large saucepan over high heat, bring the water, sugar, vanilla bean, cinnamon sticks, and anise to a boil.

2. Reduce heat to low, and add the pears.

3. Simmer for 15 to 20 minutes or until the pears are tender but not falling apart.

4. Remove the pears from the liquid with a slotted spoon or a spider, and place them in a shallow dish. Do not use tongs.

5. Boil the liquid until it has reduced to a syrup, about 15 to 20 minutes. Then stir in the lemon juice.

6. Pour the syrup over the pears, and let cool to room temperature.

7. Cover the dish, and refrigerate for at least 2 hours or overnight.

8. Serve the pears chilled, garnished with fresh lemon slices and mint leaves.

THE FORGE INN

KED BARDU, DRY STEPPES

North of Kehjistan stretches an expanse of arid grasslands, stippled with rocky canyons and salt flats. A land of scarcity even before the arrival of Barbarian tribes, here lives are worth less than whatever water can be found. The primary routes of travel are dangerous, compounded by bandits, mercenaries, and even cannibals lurking out of sight, eagerly awaiting their next meal.

The only locale in the Dry Steppes established enough to support a passable tavern is the capital of Ked Bardu. Once a simple encampment, Ked Bardu seems to have sprung from the land itself after the barbarian Oxen Tribe put down roots with their great forge. There, a local guest house known simply as the Forge Inn crafts equally legendary fare: The innkeeper, Udol, does things with braised and stewed lamb that would impress even the likes of my skilled mother. With Udol's help, I have done my best to reproduce his recipes in the pages that follow.

UDOL'S "HANDS" PIE

If there is one shred of advice that I can offer new visitors new to the Forge Inn, it is this: Beware Udol's dark wit. The innkeeper finds his silver linings in faces . . . fresh targets to shock and surprise with his jests. Indeed, during my last visit, Udol overheard a traveler harrowed by the news of cannibal sightings in the area. A mischievous twinkle appeared in the innkeeper's eye as he delivered the woman's supper. "Our hand pies are a local favorite," he announced before leaning in with a roguish grin, *"Hands delivered fresh, just this morning!"* The woman turned pale and bolted outside—so fast that Udol did not even have a chance to reveal the dish's complete absence of meat.

Difficulty: Artisan
Prep/Cook: 1 hour, 15 minutes
Yield: 6 pies

FILLING

2 tablespoons olive oil
1 medium onion, diced
  (about 1 cup)
2 garlic cloves, minced
½ medium butternut squash,
  peeled and diced (about 2 pounds)
1 teaspoon dried thyme
1 teaspoon dried sage
1 tablespoon table salt
½ tablespoon white pepper
3 tablespoons goat cheese,
  crumbled

PASTRY

2 cups all-purpose flour
½ teaspoon table salt
1 teaspoon sugar
1 cup unsalted butter, chilled
  and cubed
¼ to ½ cup ice water

EGG WASH

1 large egg
1 tablespoon milk

TO MAKE THE FILLING:

1. Preheat oven to 400°F. Line a baking sheet with parchment paper.

2. In a large skillet, heat the olive oil over medium heat.

3. Add the onion, and cook until softened, about 5 minutes. Add the garlic, and cook for 1 minute.

4. Add the butternut squash, thyme, sage, salt, and pepper.

5. Cook until the squash is tender, about 15 to 20 minutes. Remove from heat, and set aside to cool. The squash should be soft.

6. When cooled, add in the goat cheese.

TO MAKE THE PASTRY:

7. In a large bowl, whisk together the flour, salt, and sugar.

8. Cut in the chilled butter using a pastry cutter or your fingertips until the mixture resembles coarse crumbs.

9. Gradually add in the ice water until the dough comes together in a ball.

10. Divide the dough into 2 equal portions, wrap in plastic wrap, and refrigerate for 30 minutes.

11. Roll out each dough portion on a lightly floured surface to ¼-inch thickness. Cut into 4-inch squares.

TO ASSEMBLE:

12. Spoon about 2 tablespoons of the butternut squash mixture onto one half of each square.

13. Prepare the egg wash by mixing the egg and the milk.

14. Brush the edges with the egg wash, and fold the other half of the square over the filling. Press the edges together to seal.

15. Place the hand pies onto the prepared baking sheet, and brush with the remaining egg wash.

16. Bake for 25 to 30 minutes or until the pastry is golden brown.

KOTOTA RECOVERY HUMMUS AND PITA

One evening at the Forge Inn, I met a goat farmer. A native of Farobru, a town to the north, he had made the tumultuous wagon trek across the Kotota Grasslands and found some poor missionary on the side of the road, near death. Having myself traveled that stretch, I knew it unwise to journey without the aid of a local guide. But when the farmer pointed out the poor soul he had collected—a man moaning and mumbling from exposure—I was stunned to witness the man grow more and more coherent with each bite of the hummus and pita that Udol had supplied him.

Difficulty: Apprentice
Prep/Cook: 35 minutes
Yield: 3 cups of hummus

HUMMUS

One 15-ounce can chickpeas,
  drained and rinsed
¼ cup fresh lemon juice
2 garlic cloves, minced
2 tablespoons tahini
¼ cup olive oil
½ teaspoon ground cumin
1 teaspoon table salt
Black pepper, to taste
Water, as needed

PITA CHIPS

4 large whole-wheat pitas
2 tablespoons olive oil
½ teaspoon garlic powder
½ teaspoon paprika
½ teaspoon table salt

TO MAKE THE HUMMUS:

1. In a food processor, combine the chickpeas, lemon juice, garlic, tahini, olive oil, cumin, salt, and pepper.

2. Process until smooth. If the mixture is too thick, gradually add water until the desired consistency is reached.

TO MAKE THE PITA CHIPS:

3. Preheat oven to 400°F.

4. Cut each pita into 8 wedges, and separate into 2 layers.

5. Brush the pita wedges with olive oil, and sprinkle with garlic powder, paprika, and salt.

6. Arrange the pita wedges on a baking sheet in a single layer.

7. Bake for 8 to 10 minutes or until crispy and golden brown.

8. Serve the hummus with the pita chips for dipping.

OXEN TRIBE OLIVE AND BEAN SALAD

The Forge Inn draws a spare but colorful clientele. One late afternoon, before the evening crowd shuffled in, I sat at the bar detailing newly-learned recipes when a shadow loomed over me. I turned to find a scowling man—a barbarian from the look of his garb and sheer size. "The usual," he grumbled to Udol, who returned shortly with an olive and bean salad. The barbarian attacked his salad with impressive efficiency, scooping out practically half the dish, and swallowing it without chewing. "I'll get what he's having," I told Udol. "Ah, a favorite among my patrons of the Oxen tribe. Excellent choice," Udol replied with a smile before vanishing into the kitchen. In moments, I was enjoying my own olive and bean salad. When the barbarian finished, he looked at the little left of mine. Gazing at his large axe, I slid the plate his way, despite being tempted to lick up every last bit.

Difficulty: Apprentice
Prep/Cook: 25 minutes
Yield: 8 servings

3 tablespoons table salt
1 pound fresh green beans
1 quart ice
1 quart water
2 tablespoons olive oil
4 teaspoons fresh lemon juice
2 teaspoons Dijon mustard
1 teaspoon garlic powder
1 teaspoon white pepper
½ cup pitted kalamata olives, cut in half
1 small red onion, diced large
1 cup feta cheese, crumbled
3 tablespoons white balsamic vinegar
1 teaspoon dried oregano

1. Bring a medium-size pot of water to boil, and add salt.

2. Cut the green beans into bite-size pieces, about one inch in length. Place the ice and water in a bowl to make an ice bath.

3. Place the green beans in the boiling water, and cook for 2 minutes. Remove, and then place in the ice-water bath for 4 minutes to "shock" the green beans.

4. In a large bowl, add oil, lemon juice, mustard, garlic powder, and white pepper, and mix generously for about 2 minutes.

5. Add in the green beans, olives, onions, feta, balsamic vinegar, and oregano, and gently mix the ingredients together to meld the flavors.

6. Cover, and place in the fridge for at least 30 minutes to marinate. Then serve.

ORBEI MONASTERY LAMB STEW

Udol tells me that his lamb stew recipe dates back decades ago, to an era when Zakarum tenets held significant sway over the Dry Steppes. Today, followers of the Zakarum Church still traverse the arid grasslands seeking the Orbei Monastery, once a center of study for priests but now a holy ruin. This pilgrimage often includes a swing through Ked Bardu for a traditional feast at the Forge Inn.

Difficulty: Journeyman
Prep/Cook: 3 hours
Yield: 4 to 6 servings

1½ pounds boneless lamb shoulder, cut into 1-inch cubes

Table salt, to taste

Black pepper, to taste

2 tablespoons olive oil

1 large onion, diced (about 1 cup)

3 tablespoons unsalted butter

3 tablespoons all-purpose flour

8 garlic cloves, minced

1 cup red wine

1 cup chicken or lamb stock

2 sprigs fresh rosemary

2 sprigs fresh thyme

3 large turnips, diced ½ inch thick

2 carrots, peeled and diced in ½-inch pieces

2 parsnips, peeled and diced into ½-inch pieces

1 cup frozen peas

1. Season the lamb cubes with salt and pepper. In a large heavy-bottomed pan, heat the olive oil over medium-high heat.

2. Add the lamb cubes, and brown on all sides, about 5 to 7 minutes per side.

3. Remove from pan, and set aside.

4. In the same pan, reduce heat to medium and add the onion. Cook until softened, about 5 minutes.

5. Add in the butter, and melt; then stir in the flour to make a quick roux. Cook until lightly golden brown.

6. Add the garlic, and cook for 1 minute. Then deglaze with red wine, scraping up any browned bits from the bottom of the pan. Add in the chicken or lamb stock.

7. Add the rosemary and thyme to the pan, along with lamb cubes.

8. Cover the pan, and simmer over low heat until the lamb is tender, about 90 minutes.

9. Add in the diced turnips, carrots, and parsnips. Bring to a high simmer, to begin cooking the vegetables. Cook for 20 to 25 minutes.

10. Stir in the frozen peas, and cook for an additional 5 minutes at the very end until heated through.

11. Remove from the heat and serve.

RACONTEUR'S PLIGHT LENTIL CURRY

Difficulty: Journeyman
Prep/Cook: 30 minutes
Yield: 6 to 8 servings

Transcribing a recipe that I had learned from Udol one night, a dour fellow sat beside me, despite the bar being nearly empty. He must have assumed that I was a scholar of some kind as he eyed my collection of notes . . . and so began his tale of the ruins of Qara Yisu. According to this fellow, the wretched village had once made a dark bargain to keep cannibals away . . . but as Udol delivered a dish of his red lentil curry to me, I found myself too enraptured by the meal to learn how the man's story ended.

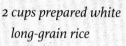

2 cups prepared white
   long-grain rice

2 tablespoons olive oil

1 large onion, diced (about 1 cup)

3 garlic cloves, minced

1 tablespoon ginger, grated

2 teaspoons ground cumin

1 teaspoon ground coriander

1 teaspoon turmeric powder

½ teaspoon cayenne pepper

One 28-ounce can diced tomatoes

2 quarts vegetable broth

1 cup red lentils, cooked,
   rinsed, and drained

1 large carrot, peeled and
   diced (about 1 cup)

1 large russet potato, peeled and
   diced small (about 1½ cups)

1 large zucchini, diced
   (about 2 cups)

One 15-ounce can chickpeas,
   drained and rinsed

Table salt, to taste

Black pepper, to taste

1 cup coconut cream

1. Cook 2 cups of white rice according to package instructions.

2. In a large saucepan, heat the olive oil over medium heat.

3. Add the onion, garlic, and ginger, and cook until softened, about 5 minutes.

4. Stir in the cumin, coriander, turmeric, and cayenne pepper, and cook for 1 minute to toast the spices.

5. Add the diced tomatoes, vegetable broth, and red lentils, and bring to a simmer.

6. Add the carrot, potato, zucchini, and chickpeas, and stir to combine.

7. Season with salt and pepper to taste.

8. Simmer until the carrots and potatoes are tender and the lentils have fallen apart, about 15 to 25 minutes. Stir occasionally to ensure nothing is sticking to the bottom of the pan.

9. When the potatoes are cooked, add in the coconut cream; stir.

10. Serve over white rice.

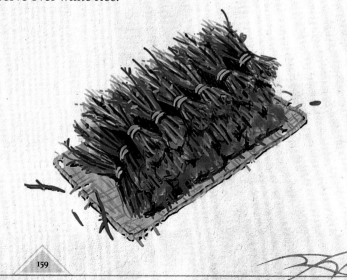

BRAISED LAMB OFFERING

Difficulty: Artisan
Prep/Cook: 3 hours, 30 minutes
Yield: 4 servings

For some time now, there have been rumors of cult activity in the shadow of Mount Civo. Udol mentioned that interest in this cult had once taken hold of a wayward barmaid who worked for him. She insisted on learning this recipe from Udol, which, he garners, must have been part of an offering that she required to gain access to the sect. Udol finally relented and shared the preparation. The next full moon, the barmaid absconded with some livestock as well as several bottles of Udol's best drink. The poor girl has not been heard from since . . . and Udol will no longer sell this dish. I have recreated it here to the best of my ability.

*1 boneless lamb shoulder
(about 3 pounds)*
Table salt, to taste
Black pepper, to taste
2 tablespoons olive oil
1 large onion, diced (about 1 cup)
3 garlic cloves, minced
1 cup chicken or lamb stock
1 cup red wine
2 sprigs fresh rosemary
2 sprigs fresh thyme

1. Season the lamb shoulder with salt and pepper.
2. In a large heavy-bottomed pan, heat the olive oil over medium-high heat. Add the lamb shoulder, and brown on all sides, about 3 to 6 minutes per side.
3. Remove from pan, and set aside.
4. In the same pan, reduce heat to medium and add the onion. Cook until softened, about 5 minutes.
5. Add the garlic, and cook for 1 minute.
6. Deglaze the pan with the chicken or lamb stock and red wine, scraping up any browned bits from the bottom of the pan.
7. Add the rosemary and thyme to the pan, and bring to a simmer.
8. Return the lamb shoulder to the pan, spooning the sauce over the top.
9. Cover the pan, and simmer over low heat until the lamb shoulder is tender, about 2 to 3 hours.
10. Remove the lamb shoulder from the pan, and keep warm.
11. Strain the sauce, and return to the pan.
12. Simmer over medium heat until the sauce has reduced and thickened slightly, about 5 to 10 minutes.
13. Serve the lamb shoulder with the reduced sauce spooned over the top.

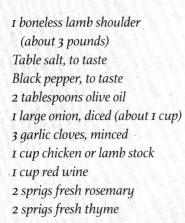

STEPPES SHORTBREAD COOKIES

Difficulty: Apprentice
Prep/Cook: 35 minutes
Yield: 20 to 24 cookies

In a land ravaged by war and devoid of growing things, you take your pleasures wherever you can get them. Years ago, the Forge Inn served an unleavened shortbread—unremarkable, by all accounts—until one day, a spice merchant stopped in for a meal. He sampled the shortbread, paused a moment, then reached into his satchel for a pouch of seasonings. Most were unknown in the Dry Steppes: anise, cardamom, and cloves, among others. He offered them to Udol and was begrudgingly paid after the innkeeper tried a taste of the adjusted recipe. The merchant now makes a monthly visit, his spices continuing to flavor the inn's splendid shortbread.

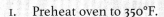

1 cup unsalted butter, room temperature
½ cup powdered sugar
2 cups all-purpose flour
¼ teaspoon table salt
1 teaspoon ground cinnamon
¼ teaspoon ground ginger
¼ teaspoon ground cardamom
¼ teaspoon ground cloves
¼ teaspoon ground allspice
¼ teaspoon ground nutmeg
¼ teaspoon ground anise

1. Preheat oven to 350°F.
2. Line a baking sheet with parchment paper.
3. In a large bowl, cream together the butter and sugar until light and fluffy.
4. In a separate bowl, whisk together the flour, salt, cinnamon, ginger, cardamom, cloves, allspice, nutmeg, and anise.
5. Gradually add the dry ingredients to the butter mixture, and mix until just combined.
6. Roll the dough into 1-inch balls, and place on the prepared baking sheet.
7. Flatten slightly with the bottom of a glass or the palm of your hand.
8. Bake for 8 to 12 minutes or until the edges are lightly golden.
9. Cool on a wire rack.

THE WITCH'S BISCUIT

ZARBINZET, HAWEZAR

I shall never forget the first words I heard about Hawezar. I was a restless boy, twining bundles of cilantro in my mother's herb shop at the bazaar. Two men were browsing our wares, and one said, "Poison, disease, and despair spread over that godforsaken land like a mold." The other fellow hacked out a jarring laugh. This was my lasting impression of Hawezar . . . until I finally braved a journey into rocky highlands and fetid swamps. The region is indeed deadly. The fauna and flora seem to share a fondness for human flesh, and the very ground emits a noxious haze. It is also a haven for cutthroats, witches, snakes, and sly merchants fencing ill-gotten goods.

Nestled within it all lies the gnat-filled village of Zarbinzet, home to the Witch's Biscuit. Named after its signature dish—biscuits smothered in spiced sausage gravy—this smoky venue provides a welcome respite from the humid air, fever dreams, and dark magic of its nearby swamplands. Fortunately its offerings are more palatable than its setting, and I have done my best to relate their preparation here.

EXILED
EGGPLANT DIP

The kitchen master at the Witch's Biscuit goes by Kilka. Some say she has Zann Esu roots in the old Kehjistani Empire, but she is cagey on the topic when confronted. I suspect she failed to return home after Emperor Hakan sealed off Caldeum, but it is not my place to pry. Nevertheless, Kilka's food is outstanding, and this eggplant dip is a prime example of her skill, regardless of her origins.

Difficulty: Apprentice
Prep/Cook: 1 hour,
30 minutes
Yield: 8 to 10 servings

2 large eggplants
  (about ½ pound)
1 tablespoon extra-virgin olive oil
2 garlic cloves, crushed
½ teaspoon tahini
½ teaspoon cumin
½ teaspoon smoked paprika
½ teaspoon table salt
¼ cup lemon juice,
  freshly squeezed
¼ cup fresh chopped parsley

1. Preheat the oven to 500°F.

2. Stab holes in the eggplants from top to bottom with a fork or a knife, and place onto a parchment-lined baking tray. Bake whole in the oven for 45 minutes until soft and melty.

3. Remove from the oven, and cool for 15 minutes. In a food processor, add the oil, garlic, tahini, cumin, paprika, salt, and lemon juice.

4. Slice the eggplants in half lengthwise, and scrape out the insides into a bowl; discard the skins. Add the eggplant to the food processor, and blend until smooth. Avoid any lumps.

5. Transfer to a bowl, and gently stir in the chopped parsley. Check for seasoning, and serve with crusty bread (page 41).

WHISPER-CHARRED OKRA

Many in Sanctuary would view charring okra pods as a waste of good vegetables. I would at one time have even counted myself among them. Rumor has it that one of the kitchen hands at the Witch's Biscuit made a twisted bargain with the Tree of Whispers to learn a slew of culinary secrets from the farthest-flung reaches of the land. While I've never found the courage to visit the Tree of Whispers myself, I'm eternally grateful to whichever individual made this dark pact in the name of flavor.

Difficulty: Apprentice
Prep/Cook: 45 minutes
Yield: 10 servings

SPICE MIX

2 tablespoons kosher salt

1 tablespoon sweet paprika

2 tablespoons smoked paprika

1½ tablespoons garlic powder

1 tablespoon ground pepper

1 tablespoon onion powder

2 teaspoons dried oregano

1 teaspoon dried thyme leaves

1 teaspoon cayenne pepper

SPICY MAYO

2 tablespoons lemon juice

1 cup mayonnaise

1 tablespoon capers, chopped

1 tablespoon maple syrup

OKRA

6 to 8 bamboo skewers (soaked)

2 pounds okra

3 tablespoons unsalted butter, melted

3 tablespoons Spice Mix

TO MAKE THE SPICE MIX:

1. Mix together salt, sweet paprika, smoked paprika, garlic powder, pepper, onion powder, oregano, thyme, and cayenne pepper. Set aside; reserve half for the mayonnaise and the other half for the okra.

TO MAKE THE SPICY MAYO:

2. In a small bowl, mix half the seasoning with lemon juice, mayonnaise, capers, and maple syrup. Set aside.

TO MAKE THE OKRA:

3. Preheat a grill or stove-top grill to 450° to 500°F.

4. Soak the bamboo skewers in water for 10 minutes.

5. Trim the okra stems and the very bottom ends.

6. Skewer 6 okra pieces through the center of each pod, alternating the direction of each piece.

7. Brush the okra with melted butter and the half of the remaining spice mix, and prepare to grill.

8. Grill the okra until browned, about 2 to 3 minutes per side. Be sure to keep flipping them, to avoid burning.

9. Remove the okra from the skewers, and sprinkle once more with the spice mix.

10. Serve with the spicy mayo dipping sauce.

ROUSED CRUSADER'S SOUP

Most of the people of Zarbinzet seem to come in two types: downtrodden locals looking to eke out a living, and a wretched contingent of broken Zakarum Crusaders. The latter have found reason to question their faith in these troubling times and often turn to the drink to find an answer. When the ale looks to best these once-mighty warriors, Kilka offers an assist by way of this black bean soup. A single hearty bowl is enough to lift one's spirits and sober one's mind, even if it is just for a short while.

Difficulty: Apprentice
Prep/Cook: 35 minutes
Yield: 4 servings

---

1 tablespoon olive oil

1 large onion, diced

3 garlic cloves, minced

1 tablespoon cumin powder

1 teaspoon paprika

½ teaspoon dried oregano

¼ teaspoon cayenne pepper

4 cups vegetable broth

Two 15-ounce cans black beans,
   drained and rinsed

1 large carrot, peeled and diced

1 large red bell pepper, diced

1 cup tomato sauce

1 tablespoon fresh lime juice

Table salt, to taste

Black pepper, to taste

2 tablespoons crème fraîche

2 tablespoons thinly
   sliced scallions

1. In a large pot, heat the olive oil over medium heat.

2. Add the onion, garlic, cumin, paprika, oregano, and cayenne pepper, and cook until softened, about 5 minutes. Then add in the broth and black beans.

3. Stir in the carrot, red bell pepper, and tomato sauce, and bring to a simmer.

4. Reduce heat to low, and simmer until the vegetables are tender, about 15 to 20 minutes. Stir occasionally.

5. Remove from heat, and use an immersion blender or a regular blender to blend the soup until smooth.

6. Return the soup to the pot if using a regular blender.

7. Stir in the fresh lime juice, and season with salt and pepper to taste.

8. Garnish with crème fraîche and scallions.

WITCH'S BISCUIT AND SAUSAGE

Despite her curt manner, I consider Kilka the closest thing to a friend that one can have in Zarbinzet. This traces back to a frenetic night of shielding patrons from a bloody street brawl that ended inside the tavern. After the offenders left, Kilka and I closed shop, scrubbed the tables, and drank ale, and Kilka eventually confided in me that she had come around to this life. "Hearth and home aren't always safe," she declared, a far-off look in her eyes. "Death finds us all, no matter where we choose to hide, but I'm happy to provide respite where I can." This dish—simple biscuits, sausage, and gravy—exemplifies that ethos.

Difficulty: Artisan
Prep/Cook: 1 hour, 30 minutes
Yield: 8 servings

BISCUITS

1½ cups all-purpose flour

1¾ teaspoons baking powder

¼ to ½ teaspoon table salt

8 tablespoons cold unsalted butter

½ cup cold whole milk, plus more as needed

2 tablespoons unsalted butter for melting

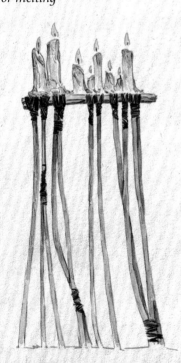

TO MAKE THE BISCUITS:

1. Preheat the oven to 400°F.

2. Line a baking sheet with parchment paper or a silicone mat, or grease with cooking spray.

3. In a large bowl, add the flour, baking powder, and salt. Whisk until blended.

4. Remove the cold butter from refrigerator or freezer, and dice into ⅛-inch cubes.

5. Spread the cold butter into the flour mix. Using a pastry blender or your fingertips, cut/rub the butter until you're left with coarse, cornmeal-like crumbs.

6. Slowly drizzle the milk into the bowl. Using a large wooden spoon, mix and fold until the mixture comes together; it should look a bit sticky. Adjust with more flour or milk as needed.

7. Using 2 large metal spoons, or by grazing your hands through the dough, make mounds of dough about 4 tablespoons in size, about the size of a lime. Drop each biscuit on the prepared baking sheet, with about ¼ inch of space between them.

8. Bake for 12 minutes in a convection oven or 15 minutes for a conventional oven, until the biscuits are a pale brown.

9. Melt the remaining butter.

10. Remove the biscuits from the oven, and brush with the melted butter; then place them back in the oven for 3 to 5 minutes until the tops are golden.

Continued on the next page

SPICY SAUSAGE GRAVY

3 tablespoons unsalted butter

2 pounds pork sausage

2 tablespoons kosher salt

1 tablespoon red chili flakes

1 tablespoon brown sugar

1 garlic clove, minced

One 16-ounce jar white pearl
*   onions, drained and rinsed*

1 cup all-purpose flour

¼ cup white wine (or apple juice)

1 cup chicken or vegetable stock

1 sprig rosemary

1 tablespoon fresh sage,
*   chopped small*

1 bay leaf

1 cup heavy cream

2 whole shallots

⅓ cup chopped curly parsley

½ tablespoon freshly
*   cracked black pepper*

¼ cup grated Parmesan cheese

TO MAKE THE SAUSAGE GRAVY:

11. In a large, heavy sauté pan, add the butter and melt at medium-high heat.

12. Add the sausage, and sauté until browned, about 6 to 8 minutes, taking care to break apart the chunks.

13. Season with salt, chili flakes, and brown sugar. Mix until fully incorporated, and then add the minced garlic and onions.

14. Add the flour, and mix until all white granules have vanished.

15. Add the white wine, and deglaze the pan, being sure to scrape the brown bits off the bottom of the pan. Reduce the heat to medium-low, and reduce the wine to half.

16. Add the stock, rosemary sprig, sage, and bay leaf, and stir. It will start to thicken in about 6 minutes; keep stirring, to make sure nothing is sticking to the bottom.

17. Add the heavy cream. Increase the heat to high and continue stirring. When the cream comes to a boil, add the shallots and parsley. Stir gently to blend everything together.

18. Finish with freshly cracked pepper and Parmesan cheese, and serve on top of or alongside the biscuits.

CRAWFISH-SMOTHERED MARSH RICE

While it is true that the denizens of Zarbinzet tend to look down upon people living in the thick of the swamp, the few who have deigned a trip into the muggy morass will tell you the kitchens there produce some of the most flavorful dishes they have ever tasted! This offering consists of a sweet, meaty crawfish in a rich gravy with celery, onions, and bell peppers. After being spiced, the sauce is ladled over rice for a dish that will instantly take your mind off the dampness, stinging insects, and snakes that might otherwise plague your travels.

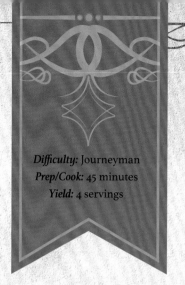

Difficulty: Journeyman
Prep/Cook: 45 minutes
Yield: 4 servings

½ cup unsalted butter

1 medium onion, chopped

½ green bell pepper,
  chopped small

½ red bell pepper, chopped small

4 celery stalks, chopped

4 garlic cloves, minced

2 teaspoons cayenne pepper

2 tablespoons paprika

2 tablespoons all-purpose flour

2 cups chicken broth

1 pound crawfish tails, peeled,
  deveined, and chopped

½ cup heavy cream

2 cups cooked white rice

Chopped fresh parsley
  for garnishing

1. In a large saucepan over medium heat, melt the butter.

2. Add the onion, both bell peppers, celery, garlic, cayenne pepper, and paprika.

3. Cook for 5 to 7 minutes or until the vegetables are tender.

4. Stir in the flour, and cook for 4 minutes.

5. Gradually whisk in the chicken broth, and bring the mixture to a boil; make sure there are no chunks.

6. Reduce heat to low, and let simmer for 10 to 15 minutes or until the mixture thickens; it should coat the back of a spoon.

7. Add the crawfish, and stir to coat. Then add the heavy cream.

8. Cook for another 5 minutes, or until the crawfish is heated through.

9. Serve the étouffée over cooked white rice, and garnish with fresh parsley.

MARAUDER'S MUJADARA

Kilka supposedly liberated this recipe, among other things, from Hawezar's lawless coastal settlement of Backwater: a haven for pirates, thieves, and smugglers of ill-gotten goods. The way Kilka tells it, she traveled there to collect a shipment of rare spices plundered from some hapless trade lord's vessel. The scoundrel with whom she was bargaining had lied about the state of the goods, which were all waterlogged after their ship had run aground on a rocky shoal. Kilka, ever the professional, thanked the man for his time, and left town without complaint . . . but not before pilfering the man's personal quarters. "You must adapt to local customs when traveling," she explained with a nod.

Difficulty: Apprentice
Prep/Cook: 50 minutes
Yield: 4 servings

---

1 cup brown lentils

7 cups water, divided

1 cup long-grain rice

¼ cup olive oil

1 large onion, chopped

4 garlic cloves, minced

½ teaspoon cumin

½ teaspoon coriander

½ tablespoon table salt

⅛ teaspoon black pepper

½ medium lemon

Fresh parsley, chopped, for garnish

1. Rinse and drain the lentils.

2. In a medium saucepan, combine the lentils with 4 cups of water, and bring to a boil.

3. Reduce heat to low, and let simmer for 15 to 20 minutes or until tender.

4. In a separate large saucepan, bring 3 cups of water to a boil.

5. Add rice, and stir. Cover, and let simmer for 18 to 20 minutes or until cooked. Keep checking to make sure the rice isn't under- or overcooked.

6. In a large skillet over medium heat, heat the olive oil.

7. Add the onion, and cook for 5 to 7 minutes or until golden brown.

8. Add the garlic, cumin, coriander, salt, and pepper, and cook for another minute.

9. Add the cooked lentils to the skillet, and stir. Cook for 2 to 3 minutes. Check for seasoning.

10. In a large serving dish, spread half of the cooked rice. Spoon the lentil mixture over the rice; then spread the remaining rice on top.

11. Squeeze lemon juice over the top of the dish, and sprinkle with fresh parsley; then serve.

PISTACHIO CONSTRICTOR COOKIES

Hawezar is home to mysterious, snake-like creatures that make even the most straightforward jaunt through the wetland groves a test of one's mettle. Travelers who manage to emerge from the swamps in one piece are encouraged to stop into the Witch's Biscuit for a cup of piping-hot tea and a fresh platter of these cookies. The fresh, almost piney pistachio flavor will help you forget your woes . . . at least until you find a giant, molted snakeskin just outside the town gates.

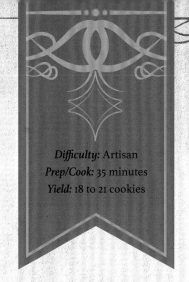

Difficulty: Artisan
Prep/Cook: 35 minutes
Yield: 18 to 21 cookies

1 cup all-purpose flour, sifted

¾ teaspoon double-acting baking powder

1 cup unsalted, shelled pistachios, ground to a fine consistency (alternatively, you can use ¼ cup pistachio flour)

½ teaspoon table salt

½ cup unsalted butter, room temperature

1 large egg

¼ cup light brown sugar

¾ cup granulated sugar

1 teaspoon vanilla extract

1 cup unsalted, shelled pistachios, chopped

½ cup powdered sugar for dusting

1. Preheat oven to 350°F. Line a baking sheet with parchment paper.
2. In a medium bowl, whisk together flour, baking powder, ground pistachios, and salt. Set aside.
3. In a large bowl, using an electric mixer, cream the butter until light and fluffy, about 2 to 3 minutes.
4. Beat in the egg, brown sugar, granulated sugar, and vanilla extract.
5. Gradually add the flour mixture to the butter mixture, and mix by hand with a rubber spatula.
6. Stir in the chopped pistachios.
7. Using a cookie scoop or spoon, form dough into 1½-inch balls.
8. Place on the prepared baking sheet about 2 inches apart.
9. Bake for 8 to 12 minutes or until the edges are lightly golden.
10. Allow the cookies to cool on the baking sheet for 5 minutes before transferring them to a wire rack to cool completely.
11. Dust the cookies with powdered sugar when cooled.

FAREWELL, TRAVELERS, AND ENJOY YOUR FARE . . .

Food is a light in the dark in these exceedingly grim times.

Lately, the darkness in Sanctuary spreads like a living murk. Roads and passes are so perilous that regional travel is reduced to a trickle, far too deadly an undertaking for most. Access to inns and taverns—the ones serving the dishes detailed herewithin—gets more difficult and dangerous every day.

I cannot in good conscience direct you to the eateries noted within—not unless you are a well-seasoned warrior or skilled mage. However, I can proffer a glimpse of these wonderful establishments . . . and then, by sharing their recipes, I can bring their incomparable kitchens to yours.

If you are one of the many brave souls who somehow manages to slip past monsters, murderers, demons, thieves, and other beasts roaming Sanctuary's reaches in order to visit one of these fine places, and the other patrons mind their manners, tell the staff that Tedric of the Table sent you. You may just get a special dish from the proprietor.

And if you do not, well . . . then I shall just have to make another visit myself one day.

Until then, comrade, happy eating and good tidings to you.

—TEDRIC OF THE TABLE

DIETARY CONSIDERATIONS

THE SLAUGHTERED CALF INN	DAIRY-FREE	GLUTEN-FREE	VEGAN	VEGETARIAN
Othyrus's Vegetable Risotto				
Old Tristram Toasted Pilaf				x
Bron's Beef Bourguignon				
Rising Sun Coq Au Vin				
Coveted Glass Noodles				
Spiced Mutton Leg and Flatbread	x			
Eira's Plum and Honey Cake				x
ATMA'S TAVERN	DAIRY-FREE	GLUTEN-FREE	VEGAN	VEGETARIAN
Sand-Swept Ceviche	x	x	x	x
Corsair Shakshuka and Crusty Bread	x		x	x
Aranoch Bay Scallops with Tarragon Cream Sauce		x		
Port Town Potato-Crusted Cod	x			
Khazra Carrots	x	x	x	x
Twin Seas Seafood Stew				
Marauder's Orange Spice Cake				x
THE CAPTAIN'S TABLE	DAIRY-FREE	GLUTEN-FREE	VEGAN	VEGETARIAN
Cheesy Hand Pie				x
Lauded Laminated Pancakes				x
Sightless Eye Ahi Tuna				
Captain's Crew Fish Stew	x	x		
Necromancer's Broiled Fish		x		
Hoodwinked Honey Carrots	x	x		x
Reshomi's Spiced Shortbread				x
WOLF CITY TAVERN	DAIRY-FREE	GLUTEN-FREE	VEGAN	VEGETARIAN
Bandit's Bacon Candy	x	x		
Essen's Spit-Roasted Pork	x	x		
Wolf City Watermelon and Spinach Salad		x		x
Longshoreman's Crab Salad Buns				
Westmarch Navy Garlic Prawns				
Wessel's Venison Stew	x	x		
Blood Marsh Chocolate Tart				x

THE SMOLDERING TONGUE	DAIRY-FREE	GLUTEN-FREE	VEGAN	VEGETARIAN
Arreat Roasted Red Pepper Eggs	x	x		x
Owl Tribe Shredded Beef	x			
Gray Wards Onion Pie				x
Harrogath Black Garlic Mushroom Roll	x			x
Ration's Respite Stir Fry	x			
Perfect Provisions Sausage Bites	x	x		
Blasphemous Apricot Cake				x
THE HANGED MAN	DAIRY-FREE	GLUTEN-FREE	VEGAN	VEGETARIAN
Osso's Jerky and Sprouts		x		
Iskren's Jerky Dip		x		
Monk's Sausage and Apple Tithe				
Pilgrim's Mushroom and Carrot Pottage				x
Knights Penitent Pork Cutlets				
Lacuni's Sacrifice Sticky Baked Chicken	x			
Snowmelt Ricotta Pancakes				x
THE BLACK GULL TAVERN	DAIRY-FREE	GLUTEN-FREE	VEGAN	VEGETARIAN
Werebear Salmon Cakes and Túr Dúlra Bread				
Frozen Sea Steamed Mussels		x		
Tavish's Kedgeree		x		
Forefather's Venison Meatballs				
Túr Dúlra Salt and Pepper Chicken and Firebreak Braised Greens				
Highlands Rabbit Fricassee				
Hinterland Poached Pears	x	x	x	x
THE FORGE INN	DAIRY-FREE	GLUTEN-FREE	VEGAN	VEGETARIAN
Udol's "Hands" Pie				x
Kotota Recovery Hummus and Pita	x		x	x
Oxen Tribe Olive and Bean Salad		x		x
Orbei Monastery Lamb Stew				
Raconteur's Plight Lentil Curry	x	x	x	x
Braised Lamb Offering	x	x		
Steppes Shortbread Cookies				x

DIETARY CONSIDERATIONS (CONTINUED)

THE WITCH'S BISCUIT	DAIRY-FREE	GLUTEN-FREE	VEGAN	VEGETARIAN
Exiled Eggplant Dip	x	x	x	x
Whisper-Charred Okra		x		x
Roused Crusader's Soup	x	x	x	x
Witch's Biscuit and Sausage				
Crawfish-Smothered Marsh Rice				
Marauder's Mujadara	x	x	x	x
Pistachio Constrictor Cookies				x

CONVERSION CHARTS

VOLUME

U.S.	METRIC
⅕ teaspoon (tsp)	1 ml
1 teaspoon (tsp)	5 ml
1 tablespoon (tbsp)	15 ml
1 fluid ounce (fl. oz.)	30 ml
⅕ cup	50 ml
¼ cup	60 ml
⅓ cup	80 ml
3.4 fluid ounces	100 ml
½ cup	120 ml
⅔ cup	160 ml
¾ cup	180 ml
1 cup	240 ml
1 pint (2 cups)	480 ml
1 quart (4 cups)	0.95 liter

WEIGHT

U.S.	METRIC
0.5 ounce (oz.)	14 grams
1 ounce (oz.)	28 grams
¼ pound (lbs.)	113 grams
⅓ pound (lbs.)	151 grams
½ pound (lbs.)	227 grams
1 pound (lbs.)	454 grams

TEMPERATURES

FAHRENHEIT	CELSIUS
200°	93°
212°	100°
250°	120°
275°	135°
300°	150°
325°	165°
350°	177°
400°	205°
425°	220°
450°	233°
475°	245°
500°	260°

ABOUT THE AUTHORS

ANDY LUNIQUE

They say life is more fun if you play games, and food tastes better with company. If you had to explain Andy Lunique's character, those traits would be the foundation of his build. With a long career in hospitality and his current role in the gaming industry, Chef Andy Lunique has managed to find ways to bridge the gap between food and gaming no matter where he is.

RICK BARBA

Rick Barba is one of the most published book authors in the video game industry, with more than 130 game-related titles in print, including *Diablo III: The Official Limited Edition Strategy Guide* and the novel *XCOM 2: Escalation* (Insight, 2017). A graduate of the Iowa Writers' Workshop, Rick has been on the writing faculty at Santa Clara University and the University of Nebraska Omaha, and has published fiction in numerous literary journals such as *Chicago Review*, *Black Warrior Review*, *AQR*, and Gordon Lish's *The Quarterly*. He's thrilled that the content of his two Starfleet Academy novels (*The Delta Anomaly* and *The Gemini Agent*) is part of the official Star Trek canon. Rick lives just outside Boulder, Colorado.

INSIGHT
EDITIONS

PO Box 3088
San Rafael, CA 94912
www.insighteditions.com

Find us on Facebook: www.facebook.com/InsightEditions
Follow us on Twitter: @insighteditions
Follow us on Instagram: @insighteditions

ISBN: 979-8-88663-132-6

Publisher: Raoul Goff
VP, Co-Publisher: Vanessa Lopez
VP, Creative: Chrissy Kwasnik
VP, Manufacturing: Alix Nicholaeff
VP, Group Managing Editor: Vicki Jaeger
Publishing Director: Mike Degler
Art Director: Catherine San Juan
Executive Editor: Jennifer Sims
Associate Editor: Sadie Lowry
Managing Editor: Maria Spano
Senior Production Editor: Katie Rokakis
Production Manager: Deena Hashem
Senior Production Manager, Subsidiary Rights:
    Lina s Palma-Tenema

Photography by Ted Thomas
Food & Prop Styling by Elena P. Craig
Assistants: Lauren Tedeschi and Wesley Anderson

Additional photography by Waterbury Publications, Inc.
Cover background photograph by Evgeny Baranov

BLIZZARD ENTERTAINMENT

Director, Consumer Products, Publishing: Byron Parnell
Associate Publishing Manager: Derek Rosenberg
Director, Manufacturing: Anna Wan
Direct Manufacturing Project Manager: Chanee' Goude
Senior Director, Story and Franchise Development: Venecia Duran
Senior Producer, Books: Brianne Messina
Associate Producer, Books: Amber Thibodeau
Senior Manager, Editorial: Chloe Fraboni
Senior Editor: Eric Geron
Senior Brand Artist, Books: Corey Peterschmidt
Senior Manager, Lore: Sean Copeland
Senior Producer, Lore: Jamie Ortiz
Associate Producer, Lore: Ed Fox
Associate Historian: Madi Buckingham, Courtney Chavez,
    Damien Jahrsdoerfer, Ian Landa-Beavers
Creative Consultation: Alanna Carroll, Mac Smith
Lore Consultation by: Madi Buckingham, Ian Landa-Beavers

Manufactured in China by Insight Editions

10 9 8 7 6 5 4 3 2 1